Venice & Food

SALLY SPECTOR
Venice and Food

Text, illustrations and calligraphy
Sally Spector

© 1998 Arsenale Editrice

printed in Italy by
EBS- Editoriale Bortolazzi Stei
San Giovanni Lupatoto (Verona)

first edition
April 1998

ISBN 88 7743 173 3

Venice & Food

written & illustrated by
Sally Spector

KILO
3 000

SAROTE
NOVELLE

CAVALLINO
7 500

BIETINA
NOSTRANA

arsenale editrice

MARE
ADRIATICO

PORTO DI LIDO

PORTO DI
MALAMOCCO

PORTO DI
CHIOGGIA

La Laguna di Venezia
1 VENEZIA
2 GIUDECCA
3 MURANO
4 TORCELLO
5 BURANO-MAZZORBO
6 SANT'ERASMO
7 TREPORTI
8 CAVALLINO
9 LIDO
10 PELLESTRINA
11 CHIOGGIA
12 CAMPALTO
13 SAN GIULIANO

Contents

Cicheti

this book is dedicated
to the memory of
my parents
Bernice and Philip Kaplan
and to
the past, present and future
of the Mediterranean

Cicheti

CICHETI are uniquely and typically Venetian and while they are not normally a part of home cooking, they merit special attention all the same. CICHETI are sometimes considered appetizers, or ANTIPASTI —ANTI means before, PASTO is meal— but they are not necessarily the prelude to lunch or supper. Their importance lies not just in the food itself but also in how, when and where they are eaten: with fingers and toothpicks, usually standing up, hanging around the counter where they are displayed in the numerous bars, OSTERIE, BÀCARI and TRATTORIE that offer them virtually all day long. They may be as simple as olives or hard-boiled eggs or as unusual as certain seafoods found only in the lagoon area, but whatever they consist of, they are the basis of a particularly Venetian ritual that takes place countless times every day: that is, ANDARE A CICHETI —to go for a nibble of this and that, accompanied by a glass of red or white wine. Yet, as ubiquitous and intrinsic as they are to Venice, since they are not part of a restaurant meal, many visitors do not experience them. Going-for-CICHETI is generally done in company but the single person is rarely alone because eating them is as much a social activity as a gastronomic one. Although they may be eaten at virtually any hour, the traditional CICHETI times are late morning (lunch is often not 'til 1:30 or 2) and early evening, before going home for supper.

PONTE DE LA MALVASIA
Canale de la Sensa,
Cannaregio
MALVASIA is a
modification of
MONEMVASIA, a
tiny island off
the south east tip
of the Peloponnesus,
famous for its violets
+ the strong, sweet
white wine made there,
called MALMSEY, or
MALVASIA. In spite of its
minute size, its strategic
position made it the "guardian" of the western entrance to the Aegean Sea + was often fought over.
It was a Venetian possession from 1464-1540. In Venice, MALVASIA was not only this wine, often drunk with
sweet biscuits; it was also the term for an OSTERIA, or tavern, that sold wine imported from overseas. The
MALVASIE were the most "refined" of the various types of public establishments that offered predominantly wine.

The word CICHETO has its origins in French. The Italian word CICCHETTARE means to drink several glasses of wine and CICCHETTO is a small glass of wine or liqueur; both derive from the French word CHIQUER, which is a glass of wine. Venetians do not drink their CICHETI, they chew them, and instead, have a very special name for the glass of wine that goes with these snacks.

In Venice, a glass of wine is not just UN BICCHIERE DI VINO — it is UN'OMBRA, meaning shade or shadow. The phrase, " to drink a shadow", or "BERE UN'OMBRA", owes its origins to the Bell Tower of San Marco and the shadow it casts in the Piazza. In the past, Piazza San Marco was full of vendors of all sorts of things, including a wine seller at the foot of the massive CAMPANILE. As the day wore on, he would adjust his awning in order to stay in its shadow, out of the sun, and "Let's go in the shade" became a way of saying "Let's have a glass of wine." The movable wine shop is no more, but the tradition of drinking a glass of wine in the shadow of the tower left its sign in this singularly Venetian idiom: UN'OMBRA is not wine drunk with a meal; it is the wine one has between meals or with CICHETI, ordered by the glass. Although today ENOTECHE, or wine bars, offer vintage Italian wines, UN'OMBRA is usually just ordinary generic red or white, "on tap." Venetians have always drunk more wine than most other Italians, jokingly said to have been due to the scarcity of fresh water here.

Venice is presently witnessing a new development in its CICHETI culture. Many Venetians now in their late twenties and early thirties grew up thinking that going for CICHETI was old-fashioned and they wanted to try new things like drinking beer. But this interest waned. It is difficult to know whether their "discovery" of this custom encouraged new places to open or if, instead, such places themselves have provoked a re-birth of this habit. In any case, it is a welcome phenomenon, especially because many of this city's traditional neigh-borhood bars and OSTERIE have disappeared in the past twenty years. In Venice, where the overwhelming presence of tourists has a negative effect on eating establishments, they were virtually the only places that continued to cater to the locals. The new CICHETI bars are not mere copies of the old ones, which usually were run by people over a certain age and, while there was nothing pro-hibiting them from going there, most young women would not have done so, alone or with other females. Many of the new proprietors are under thirty; their bars are still tiny, often tucked away in a seemingly secret corner of the city, but their atmosphere is different and women feel perfectly comfortable going to them. Some-times "foreign" things like stuffed olives or fried rice balls are offered with traditional CICHETI, but even if such things are found elsewhere, in no other place are they eaten as CICHETI.

Eating CICHETI seems inextricably tied to Venice's pedestrian way of life. Walking is like breathing here: everyone does it, must do it, every day. The city is small and things are close together; stores, offices, homes, workshops, banks, the city's university, are all densely inter-woven and it is natural for people to run into each other, stop to chat for a moment and then prolong the con-versation, going into the nearest bar to have something. There are few, if any, other cities where the CICHETO ritual could take place. One cannot go for CICHETI in a car.

BELL TOWER OF SAN MARCO
detail from the painting "Piazza San Marco" by Canaletto (1697-1768) in the Thyssen Collection, Castagnola (Lugano) Switzerland

The choice of CICHETI varies from bar to bar and may also depend on the time of year, the hour of the day and the type of clientele that frequent a place. They are essentially a "popular", "people's" food and are often made from inexpensive ingredients. Thus, some of the most traditional ones are internal organs, one of the most common being NERVETTI, or the nerves of a calf or cow: boiled and chopped, they are off-white in color, smooth, with an almost translucent aspect and a soft consistency.

The POLPETTA is another typical CICHETO. It is a flattened meatball, about two inches across, breaded and fried in butter or lard and usually eaten cold; its specific contents often depend on the fantasy of the cook and whatever leftovers are available — it is said to have been born in order that nothing edible was thrown away. William Dean Howells (1837-1919), who was sent by President Abraham Lincoln to be the American Consul in Venice from 1861-1865, described his experience here in his book, Venetian Life, first printed in 1872. Of POLPETTE he wrote: "I confess a tenderness for this dish which is a delicater kind of hash skillfully flavored and baked (sic) in rolls of a mellow complexion and fascinating appearance." His words remain valid.

BACALÀ is codfish that has been preserved by drying it in the open air and then salting it; fresh cod is MERLUZZO. Venetians make BACALÀ MANTECATO which is creamed dried cod. The BACALÀ is soaked in water, boiled, and then vigorously pounded or beaten with olive oil added drop by drop until the mixture becomes very soft, almost whipped and foamy; it also contains garlic, pepper and parsley. It is normally eaten with POLENTA: a spoonful of white BACALÀ is heaped on a little square of toasted or grilled yellow POLENTA and while it is very good at room temperature, it is excellent slightly warmed (p.144).

There are numerous references to CICHETI in this book and new interest in such things as vegetarian cooking and ethnic foods means that the variety of these snacks is constantly growing.

Sally Spector

typical ceramic pitcher used for wine in Venice

Water & Wells

Acqua e Pozzi

Water, essential in cooking, was always extremely precious for Venetians. It surrounds and penetrates their city and is an integral part of its beauty, charm and mystery; virtually every aspect of life here is in some way conditioned by its presence. In the past, this water protected Venetians, for the lagoon encircled them like the stone walls that other cities built to keep out invaders, but it also threatened their very survival due to the flooding that has always plagued Venice. None of this water, however, is drinkable. The lagoon, created by the constant interaction between the Adriatic Sea and the rivers that empty into it, is salty.

At first, Venice's fresh water came from a few wells whose subsoil naturally accumulated rain water, but by the late 10th century they no longer met the city's growing needs. To have the fresh water necessary to sustain life, Venetians developed an ingeneous system of underground cisterns —called POZZI, or wells— that collected, purified and stored rain water, recognized by their beautiful stone VERE DA POZZO, known as "well-heads".

These wells were very costly to build; their size depended on the space available —a public square or private court— and estimates of average daily rainfall. A four-sided opening was dug, five or six meters deep, and its walls and floor were layered with impermeable clay. A "tube" of bricks was erected in its center on a slab of Istrian stone, the white, non-porous limestone from the Istrian peninsula used for structural, sculptural and decorative purposes all over Venice. The cistern was then completely filled with river sand which cleaned and filtered the rain water that entered through small holes at its four corners; a crucial part of the well, these holes had to be kept free of anything that could clog them but they also had to be plugged in the event of high tides since the salty flood water could damage and even ruin the POZZO and contaminate its contents, encouraging the spread of infection and disease. Lastly, a brick or stone pavement was laid over the cistern, slightly inclined to facilitate

Sally Spector

WELL-HEAD, 15th cent., in Campo del Ghetto Novo, Cannaregio, decorated with three lions of Judah.

the water's accumulation, or raised a bit above street level for greater volume. These pavements and the gutters on surrounding buildings also played a part: by law, their water had to drain through pipes into the wells, to eventually be drawn out of the meter-wide brick "tube" in the center.

Periodic droughts and population growth meant that, again, wells could not satisfy Venice's needs and in 1386, one of the city's most humble, fatiguing and important occupations was established: the AQUAROLI, who brought water from nearby rivers. They filled BURCHI, robust boats used for transporting heavy loads, like sand, which held from 9,000 to 18,000 liters and rowed them to Venice. As the official water suppliers, for both industrial and domestic use, they sold buckets of it on the street and made sure that no commercial activity- no barbers, tripe sellers, glass makers, cloth dyers, etc., used free, public well water —if they did so, they had to donate an entire BURCHIO to the abused well. While the AQUAROLI alleviated the problem of an adequate supply of drinking water, they could not resolve it, for Venice's needs continued to increase. In the 1300's, building a canal from the River Brenta, famous for its pure, sweet water, was considered and in the first quarter of the 1600's the Seriola Veneta was created: running parallel to the river, it was fed with Brenta water that entered through a sophisticated filtering system and scrupulously controlled to guard against any possible pollution —people could not even walk along its banks. BURCHI brought this water, filling Venetians' wells and buckets, for another 250 years.

Most people got water from the public wells built by the State while the wealthy, and religious institutions had their own private ones. Strict laws regulated the use of public wells, a severity easily understood considering how important fresh water was and how precarious its supply; wasting

WELL-HEAD, c. 1350-1450, in Corte de la Pagola near Santi Apostoli, Cannaregio

water was almost a crime in Venice. Twice daily, at the ringing of a special bell, district officials unlocked and opened the wooden well covers and people, usually women, would gather, chatting and gossiping while waiting to fill their buckets. The POZZI provided more than just water; they were the basis for a ritual that was a lively, fundamental and often pleasing part of daily life. For those who could afford it, additional water was available from BIGOLANTI, peddlers who went to homes and stores selling small quantities of it: a BIGOLO is the curved wooden yoke with a bucket at both ends that these vendors, for the most part women, balanced on their shoulders as they went from door to door. Although the BIGOLANTI, like the AQUAROLI, provided a very important service, water remained a constant concern for Venetians.

As early as the 1500's the government had considered building an aqueduct for bringing water to Venice from the terra firma but it was not seriously discussed until the early 1800's. This delay is usually explained by the fact that the city wanted to remain self-sufficient, and not dependent on the mainland for its water, for it feared the possibility that this supply could be cut off during times of conflict or war. In the 1800's, many aspects of Venetian life had greatly deteriorated; in 1874, for example, only 1,907 of the city's 5,339 wells had clean, drinkable water and repeated cholera epidemics and degraded living conditions were in part caused by this unhealthy situation. The first step towards a solution was an aqueduct built under the lagoon to bring Brenta water from the mainland to cast-iron fountains constructed for this new system. Thus, 1884, the AQUAROLI were eliminated and the wells were capped with the heavy iron covers seen today. But, river water no longer satisfied modern hygienic requirements.

To comply with new health standards, a better source was sought: at Sant'Ambrogio di Grion, about 30 kms. north of Venice, perfectly clean, transparent water was found at 16 meters below ground. By 1890 this water was running in an underground aqueduct on the mainland that hooked up with the earlier one under the lagoon, later enlarged and extended to Murano and the Giudecca. In the early 1900's more and more homes had running water and the fountains were no longer necessary, though many of them still function. The water from Sant'Ambrogio is what Venetians drink today; its source is completely underground —it contains no purified river water— and is exceptionally delicious and perfectly safe to drink right from the tap. In fact, it is said that certain foods here, like POLENTA, in which water is an important ingredient, are particularly tasty because of this precious liquid.

Venice's VERE DA POZZO are among the city's most picturesque and characteristic features. In addition to the emblems of monastic orders and lay confraternities and the coats of arms of private families, a common decoration is the amphora —an obvious reference to their function- and the Lion of San Marco, the symbol of Venice's patron saint, Mark, and thus of Venice. The amphoras are still more or less visible but nearly all the lions were scraped off wells, and bridges, after the end of the Republic in 1797 because they were considered to be signs of the old, aristocratic regime. The earliest, medieval well-heads were simple, four-sided forms, while cylindrical shapes predominated from the 12th to the 14th centuries; in the 1300's and 1400's they resembled huge Romanesque capitals and the 1500's produced the most richly, lavishly ornamented ones which were followed by more classical motifs in the 1600's and 1700's. There were once more than 7,000 well-heads in Venice and its islands but only one-third of them are in their original place today. The rest are in museums, private hands and in antique dealers' galleries in Europe and North America.

CAST IRON FOUNTAIN Campiello delle Strope Similar fountains were installed throughout Venice after the wells were capped in 1884 when the aqueduct was built & were used until people had running water in their homes.

WELL-HEAD, c. 1400, in Campiello de le Strope near Campo San Giacomo da l'Orio, Santa Croce

CAMPO SAN ZANIPOLO, CASTELLO

Rice   Riso

In Venice, as everywhere else in Italy, the first course is usually the most important part of a meal. First courses -i PRIMI- are the glory of Italian cooking and an expression of this nation's great regional diversity since they differ considerably from north to center to south even though the basic ingredients remain quite similar. First courses normally bring to mind PASTA in any of its amazing shapes: today one can choose such things as PENNE (pen nibs), FARFALLE (butterflies or bow ties) or FUSILLI (spirals) in addition to the traditional SPAGHETTI (thin strings).

But this is a rather recent situation, the result of industrial production which began after World War II; PASTA is now an everyday food in Venice but it is actually very "un-Venetian" and before the 1960's was far less common than today. The only PASTA many older Venetians remember eating when they were young was an occasional bowl of TAGLIATELLE (egg noodles), SPAGHETTI or SUBIOTINI, the short form used in the famous bean soup, PASTA e FASIOI (p. 83) The real star of Venetian PRIMI is, instead, RISO, or rice.

It is generally assumed that rice originated in south-east Asia, probably China, due to the fact that various wild forms of this plant grow in swamps and bogs there and archaeological evidence shows it was being cultivated along China's eastern coast as far back as 5,000 years B.C. But, botanists and historians of agriculture distinguish between the spontaneous and the cultivated presence of plants and since a wild form of rice grows on many continents, but not in Europe, its exact birthplace is still a mystery. From China, it spread throughout south-eastern Asia to Indochina and India and then to the Middle East. Although botanists have not studied this particular group of cereals as thoroughly as, for example, wheat, it is none the less certain that all types of cultivated rice derive from the wild ones through mutation or natural cross-breeding and that they flourished best in Asia where the environment they find most favorable —swamps and bogs— is plentiful.

The ancient Greeks knew of rice — their word ORYZA is the origin of the words rice and RISO— but it was a luxury for them, imported from Syria and Egypt, used sparingly for medicinal purposes and not as food. It was important enough that the great Greek scientist and disciple of Aristotle, Theophrastus (c.370-285 B.C.), included it among the plants described in his botanical treatise Historia plantarum. Another famous Greek, Galen (129-201 A.D.), wrote of its effectiveness in treating a variety of health problems; the most important edition of his writings in the original Greek was printed in 1525 by Aldo Manuzio, Jr., in Venice, then the world's leading center of book publishing. Like the Greeks, the ancient Romans imported rice and though they began to realize its gastronomic, along with its therapeutic, qualities it remained a precious commodity, reserved for the wealthy.

Arabs introduced rice from the Middle East into North Africa and then into Spain when they invaded that country in the early 8th century. In Europe, throughout the Middle Ages and until the 1400's it remained a rarity, something imported from faraway, often unknown places. In Venice, it was sold in the SPEZIERIE, or spice shops, the forerunners of present day pharmacies, along with costly, exotic and precious things like pepper, cinnamon and cloves (p163). It was not yet con-sidered "food" but rather, medicine, and was eaten only by sick people and those with intestinal and

COLOPHON of Aldo Manuzio (1450-1515). The quality & innovation of the books he printed - for their size, type & contents make this the most famous printer's mark of all time. It was probably based on an ancient Roman coin: the anchor & dolphin symbolize reliability & speed. Manuzio's motto, from the coin, was FESTINA LENTE, or hasten slowly.

RICE
fam. Graminaceae, Oryza sativa

stomach problems; in fact, it is the most digestible of all the grains. Because it was expensive, it had symbolic value: a tiny bag of rice was sometimes given as a gift or sign of respect; moreover, since it is associated with fertility, the custom was born of throwing grains of raw rice at newly-weds after their marriage ceremony, still done in Italy today.

The Italian cultivation of rice started in Sicily, introduced in 1442 by the Aragonese who were ruling there, after which it moved into southern Italy and Tuscany and then into the regions of Piedmont

Ronchone da tagliar cespugli

and Lombardy, in northern Italy, where newly created canals offered extremely advantageous growing conditions. Venice continued its practice of importing rice, which historians suggest was due to the fact that the government made substantial profits from customs duties and import taxes and thus was not very motivated to produce it. In addition, the agricultural conditions of the Veneto were very different from those required for growing this cereal and the necessary swamps had to be created. Transforming terrain, even when uncultivated, into rice fields was very costly, entailing land drainage, irrigation and the diverting of rivers, a financial undertaking that the Venetian State was not disposed to venture.

In spite of these obstacles, a few wealthy citizens of the REPUBBLICA VENEZIANA were willing to try planting this grain. They lived near Verona, about 100 km. west of Venice —which was under its domain from 1406-1796, interrupted only by Emperor Maximillian the First's occupation of it from 1509 to 1516— and somehow they understood this area's potential for growing rice. These landowners

Fiochetto da tagliar l'herba

FARMING IMPLEMENTS *for cutting shrubs & grass from woodcuts in* Le vinti giornate dell'agricoltura et de' piaceri della villa *(The Twenty Days of Agriculture & the Pleasures of Country Life) by Agostino Gallo (1499-1570), a gentleman farmer who studied languages & science but whose greatest love was agriculture. From the edition printed in 1573 in Venice, by Camillo & Rutilio Borgomineri. (Marciana Library)*

exploited the hydraulic potential of the Basso Veronese, the lowlands to the south of Verona between the Po and the Adige Rivers, and in the 1500's began producing what became known as the "TESORO DELLE PALUDI", or the "treasure of the swamps". These agricultural private entrepreneurs were freer to take this initiative than was the State and it is presumed that they had also taken into consideration Verona's privileged geographic position: it is an important crossroads for trade, both domestic and with northern Europe, and this doubtlessly influenced their decision, which would eventually provide welcome revenue as well as one of the world's most prestigious varities of rice. But, this grain had not yet entered into Italian, or Venetian, cuisine.

It is greatly thanks to Siena-born Pier Andrea Mattioli (1500-1577) that rice began to be regarded as a significant source of nourishment even for healthy people. Trained in medicine, he is best remembered for his writings on the natural sciences, the most important one being a systematic compendium of all the information then available on medicinal botany entitled I Discorsi di M. Pietro Andrea Mattioli, Senese, Medico Cesareo... nei sei libri di Pedacio Dioscoride Anazarbeo della Materia Medicinale (Interpretation of Dioscoride's six books on medicine by Pier Andrea Mattioli, with his comments).

First published in 1544 in Venice and reprinted numerous times in the 1500's (32,000 copies had been printed in Venice by 1562), Mattioli's work was quickly translated into several languages such as German, French and Bohemian. This treatise is a commentary on the writings of Pedanius Dioscorides (1st century A.D.), who, in addition to being the physician for the Roman army during the reign of the Emperor Nero, was one of the greatest of the ancient Greek medical doctors and scientists. His herbal, De materia

RICE from the woodcut in Mattioli's Pedacio Discoride printed in Venice in 1645 by Marco Ginami (Marciana Library)

Medica Libri Quinque (Five Books on Medicine) describes the therapeutic properties of plants, which he arranged according to their characteristics and not alphabetically as his predecessors had done. His five books divide 600 plants into lubricants, spices, herbs, roots etc. and rice is one of them. Since almost all health problems were once treated with remedies made from plants, a knowledge of botany was essential for physicians and this work remained a fundamental source of information for more than 1,000 years; it circulated in manuscript form for centuries and was printed first, in Venice, in 1499. Mattioli's translation and commentary included some new material, such as his praise for the virtues of rice: easy to digest, tasty and fortifying. His style was very persuasive and as he wrote in VOLGARE, Italian instead of Latin, his work reached a wide public and served as the model for similar studies for over 200 years. Rice began to lose its medicinal connotation and was no longer associated with sick people and after 1550, perfectly healthy people began eating it, not yet on its own but rather, mixed with other cereals, like millet and rye, for making bread and porridge.

Rice was consumed as an independent food starting in the 1600's, when it was being cultivated in sufficient quantities such that it was no longer necessary to import it; it became less costly and thus even ordinary people could obtain it. Its popularity and production continually increased and by the 1700's the SERENISSIMA, as the Venetian Republic was called, was able to export some of its crop which was a very unusual situation for this state that had always depended on imported grain to feed its citizens. Rice also proved to be very important during periods of famine and when other cereals were scarce, and its cultivation greatly benefitted from certain scientific advancements that were taking place in the 18th century: new techniques in glass making, for example, improved the level, the instrument that makes it possible to select the perfectly horizontal terrain that is best for growing rice.

Although 90% of the world's rice is now grown in Asia, the Italian production is the most technically advanced and many people consider it to be the best. It grows at a higher latitude than all the other types and thus has a longer growing cycle and this, along with the particular composition of its soil, gives it a higher nutritional content: Italian rice has at least 2% more protein than Spanish and American rice. In addition, its seeds are sowed directly in the rice paddies instead of being transplanted there, as is common in other places, which also makes it better.

MEASURING WITH A LEVEL, engraving from La Coltivazione del Riso (The Cultivation of Rice) by Gian Battista Spolverini (1695-1763) printed in Verona in 1758; reprinted seven times in the 1700's & five times in the 1800's, this work is an example of a POEMA GEORGICO, or "agricultural poem"; a form used by many intellectuals in northern Italy in the 18th century when writing about agriculture. Spolverini's work discusses the best terrain for planting rice, the correct implements to use, etc. The engravings were done by Francesco Lorenzi. From the edition printed in 1763 in Verona by Agostin Carottoni. (Marciana Library)

The Veneto ranks third in Italian rice production, after the Piedmont and Lombardy, but it is the number one consumer of it. While rice is eaten throughout northern and central Italy, except for the famous RISOTTO alla MILANESE there are very few recipes of note outside of the Veneto and it is in Venice that it receives some of its most extraordinary treatment. In this city it is always served on its own, as an independent course, never as a side dish or accompaniment to the main course and is usually cooked with vegetables, meat or fish.

There are two basic types of Venetian rice dishes: one is eaten with a spoon and is called MINESTRA — from the word MINESTRARE, meaning to serve liquidy food— and the other is eaten with a fork and is called RISOTTO, which means "rice that has completely absorbed its cooking liquid". Different qualities of rice are used for them but their main difference lies in how much or how little liquid there is in relation to the rice. The MINESTRA is BRODOSA, or brothy, while the RISOTTO is more creamy. Unfortunately, however, things are not always as clear-cut as these two categories might suggest. The word RISO is sometimes used for both, which can seem confusing to foreigners but apparently is not so for Venetians, and in other parts of Italy the term MINESTRA often refers to soups which may or may not contain rice, or even to a variety of different first courses.

In the Venetian sense, the MINESTRA consists of rice, broth and one or more vegetables. It was once very present in the Veneto and many people I know speak nostalgically of the MINESTRE of their youth, of the bowls full of hot broth with white grains of rice floating amidst whatever vegetables were in season. Today this soup is considered rather ordinary, almost plebian; restaurants do not offer it and most young people have no idea what this once so typical dish is. PASTA and the more "sophisticated" RISOTTO have replaced it but perhaps it will return some day and attain its deserved recognition. Not only is it nourishing, satisfying and delicious, it is also quite easy to make and is one of Venice's most authentic dishes. Two of the most popular ways of preparing it are described here but almost any vegetable can be adapted to the basic principle: rice and vegetable cooked together —not just mixed or added to each other— in enough liquid to be eaten with a spoon.

A RISOTTO is a bit trickier to make than a MINESTRA because it must be stirred constantly while the rice is boiling to keep it from sticking to the pot, but it is very easy to tell if it has been cooked correctly. The grains become transluscent, alabaster-like, each one surrounded by a creamy coating that unites them all into a tender mass. They do not stick or clump together; when gathered onto a fork, they do not fall off.

To make these dishes properly, in order for them to be genuinely Venetian, Italian rice must be used. Italian rice is short grain: it has a stubby, oval form, wider and a bit paunchy around the middle and it is much harder than long grain. Its nucleus is very rich in starch, which gives Italian rice dishes their characteristic creamy consistency and requires cooking at a very high temperature (boiling) so that this starch can be released. There are three main types: COMUNE or ORIGINARIO, for MINESTRE, salads and sweets, SEMI-FINO for molds and FINO or SUPER-FINO for RISOTTI, whose grains are harder than the other two and so they must be cooked a bit longer. Because the RISOTTO rice absorbs virtually all of its cooking liquid, this dish is normally eaten with a fork.

Venetians, in fact, were the first modern Europeans to eat with a fork and they were using it well before rice entered their cuisine. The history of the table fork is rather difficult to ascertain since very few examples from the remote past exist, unlike the numerous knives and spoons that archaeological research has revealed. Its function was a bit different from today: instead of forks as we now know them, used for bringing food from a plate up to one's mouth, during antiquity, fork-like objects were employed mostly for cutting and serving food. This was done for the ancient Romans by the SCISSOR, who was the official in charge of slicing and portioning out meat and other foods since very few people had their own knives, for which one of his utensils was a two-pronged instrument, similar in shape to a tuning fork. It is imagined that when the Roman Empire was in its most decadent phase, something like a fork may have been popular since this utensil is often associated with excessive, exaggerated refinement. But, most of the time people were satisfied with picking up food with their hands, and since soups were drunk, from bowls, and food was not consumed hot, it was easy to handle it. Such table manners were considered normal, completely acceptable in all situations, and they continued to be so for centuries.

The Byzantine Empire (395-1453), whose court was notorious for its great luxury and extravagance, used the fork, and it was a Byzantine princess, Theodora, who introduced it to Venice. She married this city's 31st Doge, Domenico Selvo (1071-1084) and brought a fork with her here: solid gold, with two prongs. At first, her unusual dining behaviour scandalized the Venetians, who thought eating with it was a decadent affectation, superfluous because hands worked perfectly well for this purpose.

But, with time, it was accepted and even ordinary Venetians were eating with a fork well before the rest of Europe, in spite of the fact that some clergymen said it was a creation of the devil.

Theodora's origins can be seen in the legacy she left: the Venetian word for fork is PIRON, the same as the Greek word for it, which was the language of the Byzantine Empire. In Italian, it is FORCHETTA, from the Latin word FURCA, meaning pitchfork.

BYZANTINE CAPITAL from north façade of the Basilica di San Marco, 11-12th century

For several centuries the rest of Europe considered eating with a fork to be a Venetian custom. In the second half of the 1500's the French King, Henry III, son of Catherine de' Medici, introduced it to his court but it remained virtually unknown in England until the writer, Thomas Coryat (1577-1617), returned home from his travels in Europe in 1608. The famous account of this trip, printed in London in 1611 as CORYAT'S CRUDITIES, Hastily gobled up in Five Months Travells in France, Savoy, Italy etc., was the first English guide to the Continent and includes a description of his discovery of the fork when he was in Venice. He brought one back to London where he persisted in eating with it in spite of the laughter that it provoked from his friends.

Venetians have their "own" silverware pattern, called SAN MARCO, which one often sees in private homes and in the windows of silver shops. Its design is quite simple, distinguished by the three-lobed shape at the end of the handle, the three-pronged fork and the curved tip of the knife, said to be based on the official Doge's cap. SAN MARCO silverware dates back at least to the 1700's; while today's forks have shorter prongs, spaced a bit farther apart than in the past, the pattern is otherwise unchanged.

I do not like to insist that visitors to Venice do one thing or another, but eating RISOTTO is close to obligatory. It usually must be ordered for at least two people, but a few TAVOLE CALDE, which are like cafeterias, serve single portions... not the "real thing" because prepared in large quantities, in advance, but still worth trying.

DOGE'S CAP from the portrait of Doge Leonardo Loredan (1501-1521) by Giovanni Bellini (1430-1516) in the National Gallery, London

ARCHWAY OF THE
COVERED PASSAGEWAY
that leads to the

SOTOPORTEGO E CORTE DEI FORNI

"courtyard of the bread ovens", near Santa Sofia, Cannaregio

One of the things that always struck me when I used to visit Italy was the presence of food — the actual article, not the eating establishments. It seemed as if there was always a tiny fruit and vegetable store nestled amidst the majestic buildings or an outdoor stand, full of artfully arranged produce protected by a green canvas awning. Bakers, butchers, cheese and salami shops were all part of the historic cityscape and had very often been occupying their premises for just as long as the architectural monuments around them. But, much has changed in the past decade for, more and more, the European Union, industrial production, supermarkets and demographic shifts are affecting where and how Italians buy food today. Venice, like other places in Italy, has been subject to these influences.

Every district in Venice had one or more bakers of bread, depending on the number of its inhabitants. While all other types of food could be sold in the CAMPI — the Venetian term for public squares, CAMPO means field — bakers were prohibited. They could make & sell bread only in the side streets, or CALLI. Perhaps the Venetian government wished to avoid the social unrest that other European cities often experienced: bread was an essential food & bread riots were not uncommon. Public disorder could be prevented & controlled more easily in short, narrow streets than in large open spaces, & in fact, no such event ever occurred in Venice.

Today, some of the CAMPI have bread shops.

While some of these changes have brought improvements, they have also caused many of the little, family-run neighborhood grocery stores to disappear and even before their demise, many other edible things, often sold by street vendors and peddlars, were eliminated. But, while there is no substitute for them, Venice offers something that keeps their memory alive and amuses the imagination: street names. The toponomy for CALLI, FONDAMENTA, SOTOPORTECHI, CANALI, PONTI and CORTI (streets, covered passageways, canals, bridges and courtyards), of which there are hundreds, almost always refer to something historical; they may be named for a family or person who once lived there, they may have a religious connotation or indicate a trade or profession once carried out in that place, and they are very often associated with food and related occupations. Thus, they draw a picture of gastronomic life and suggest the lively activity, and perhaps even sounds and odors, that once filled the narrow streets. The repetition of certain ones is a sign of their importance and it is not surprising that there is a total of 79 references to bread located throughout the city, and but one place named for oysters — OSTRICHE in Italian— near Campo Santa Maria del Giglio or Zobenigo.

FONDAMENTA DE LE OSTREGHE

CALLE DE L'OGIO O DEL CAFETIER

STREET of OIL or of the CAFFÈ, near the Scuola Grande di San Giovanni Evangelistic, San Polo. There was once a deposit for storing olive oil + a coffee house in this CALLE. Introduced into Venice in 1638 from Constantinople, coffee became a very popular drink. Many Venetian CAFFÈ were also gaming houses!

Place names in Venice are written in stenciled black letters on a white background, framed by a thin black border, painted directly onto the plastered walls of the buildings. These street signs are affectionately called NIZIOLETI, which is the Venetian term for the Italian word LENZUOLA, meaning layers or sheets, especially bed linens. It is easy to see why they got this nickname for they resemble miniscule bed sheets hung out to dry, like the laundry that is so much a part of this cityscape. While the words NIZIOLETI and LENZUOLA look quite different when written, when spoken, there is an obvious connection between them.

Making Venetian

Rice Dishes

Venetian rice dishes normally start with a DESFRITO —SOFFRITTO in Italian— which means "lightly fried". The DESFRITO consists of one or more of the following, finely chopped: onion, garlic, celery, carrot and PANCETTA, or unsmoked ham, cooked very gently in a small quantity of olive oil or butter, or both, until soft. The SOFFRITTO is a fundamental part of Italian cooking and varies slightly from region to region. The Venetian version is less pronounced than elsewhere in Italy and even than that made on the nearby mainland, where lard is sometimes used.

Many people claim that it is precisely the DESFRITO which gives Venice's rice dishes their particular, delicate character. It must be cooked very gently and never let darken or burn. Venetians use only fresh vegetables for their DESFRITO and they add very few herbs or spices, relying instead on the pure and natural flavor of the ingredients.

Venetian recipes are extremely flexible and variations on them seem unlimited, often depending only on personal preference, family tradition or the fresh produce available; there seem to be as many recipes for PASTA E FASIOI (p.83) as there are grandmothers and even as classic a dish as RISI E BISI (p.54) is subject to differing opinions regarding its DESFRITO —some people add PANCETTA. Venetians show similar elasticity toward amounts of ingredients. They have difficulty indicating exact measures for they cook AD OCCHIO —by eye— using a PUGNO, or fistful, of rice and

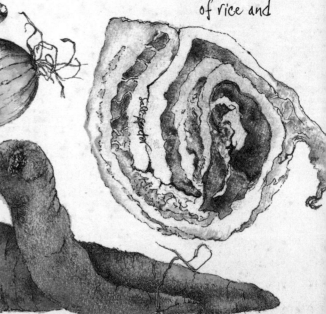

a DITO, or "finger" of wine,   UN PO DI -a bit of- butter and oil or just QUANTO
BASTA, which means, "however much is necessary." If fresh parsley would be good but
there is none, they leave it out: Venetians use fresh herbs, not dried ones. They are often rather
vague about how long things should cook; except for the 18-20 minute rule for RISOTTI, they
consider such factors as the type of pot used and how an ingredient is sliced when determining
cooking time and thus a certain liberty may be taken with the recipes in this book.

Cheese   FORMAGGIO   formagio

Today many rice dishes in Venice are served with freshly grated PARMIGIANO REGGIANO,
or Parmesan cheese. This is not traditional since in the past this cheese was a luxury, if
available at all. In fact, it was so precious that it was worthy of being offered in homage
to foreign rulers, as the Venetian Republic did to the Grand Vizier of Constantinople
during the intermittent periods of peace between them. Thanks to the greatly improved
standard of living that the Veneto now enjoys, this expensive cheese has become quite
common here. It is never served with dishes containing fish except BACALÀ ALLA VICENTINA (p.144)
and requesting it for such would be met with surprise and perhaps dismay.

PARMIGIANO REGGIANO merits this name only if it is made during the summer when cows
are outside and graze in open pastures and only if it comes from the area around the cities
of Parma, Reggio nell' Emilia (from which its name comes), Modena and Bologna in
the region of Emilia-Romagna, and Mantova, in the region of Lombardy. However,
a similar cheese is made in much of northern Italy: called GRANA PADANO, it is
a bit less expensive and extremely good. PARMIGIANO is also familiarly called
GRANA or FORMAGGIO DI GRANA with reference to its granular consistency.
Considering how costly this cheese is, it is not surprising that in jargon
'GRANA' is a term for money; less understandable is its popular
meaning of problems or trouble.

Unlike most places in Italy,
Venice has never had its own characteristic cheese,
which is not surprising, considering its lack of grazing area; it has always
been imported from the foothills of the Dolomite mountains, the region of Puglia
in the south, the island of Crete —a Venetian possession from 1204 'til the 1600's—
and from the mountainous region of Dalmatia, populated by
Morlacchian shepherds. The most "local" cheese, typical of the
Veneto, is simply called LATTERIA; it is a mild, semi-soft
cheese, made from cow's milk, or LATTE.

In 1436, Venice's cheese vendors formed a
SCUOLA —the Venetian term for a guild or
corporation— called SCUOLA DEI
CASAROLI, from the Latin CASEARUM,
which refers to butter and cheese: the
latter is called FORMAGGIO because,
unlike milk, it has a solid form. Their written
regulations stipulated that they could acquire and
sell domestic, foreign, fresh and salted cheeses and were
prohibited from using material, such as clay, to disguise
or hide signs of mold on them and it was likewise unlawful to conceal the presence of worms in them.

Cheeses were very expensive, and imported cheese was also heavily
taxed, beyond the means of ordinary people. But, for those
who could actually afford them they
were not difficult to obtain.

CORTE
DEL FORMAGER

3678

Sala Spector

CORTE DEL FORMAGER

The name of this tiny courtyard, just off Campo Santa Margherita, in Dorsoduro, near the truncated bell tower indicates the past presence of a cheese merchant. The carved wooden brackets between the columns' capitals + the architrave, called BARBACANI, were a means of adding support to a structure; BARBACANI are usually part of the additions built on to Venice's buildings in an attempt to increase their limited space, especially during the 14th + 15th centuries.

The main cheese markets were concentrated around the Rialto and San Marco but there were also tiny shops and stalls in many other parts of the city. There was even a singular traffic in this product on the Riva degli Schiavoni near the Arsenale shipyards where the CASAROLI had competition from sailors who turned what began as a privilege into a profit. On voyages back to Venice from the Eastern Mediterranean they were each allowed to bring, duty free, as much as 200 pounds of cheese, as well as oil, wine and salted meat. Although such goods were supposed to be for their families, cheese from the Peloponnesus and the type known as MORLACCO from Dalmatia were sold more or less openly on the Riva where seamen ran their own busy market.

When eating MINESTRE and RISOTTI the amount of grated cheese to use depends somewhat on personal taste, but Italians tend to use less than foreigners —just a sprinkle— for it should not smother the other flavors. It is usually served separately, from a little bowl, passed around at the table.

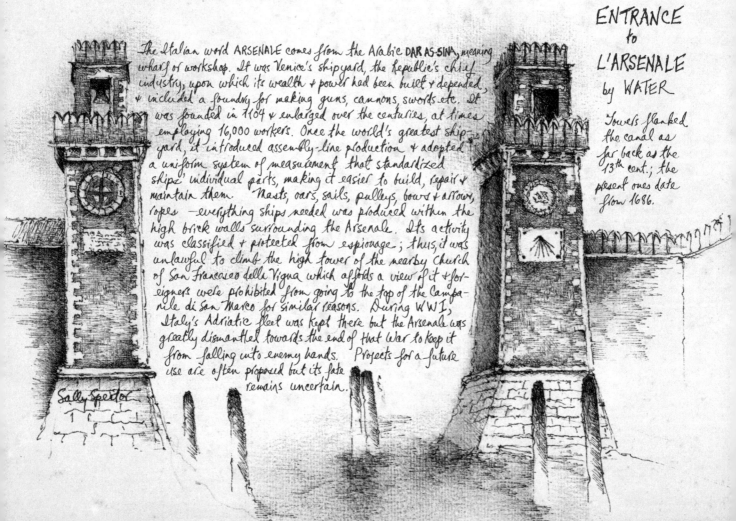

ENTRANCE to L'ARSENALE by WATER

Towers flanked the canal as far back as the 13th cent.; the present ones date from 1686.

The Italian word ARSENALE comes from the Arabic DAR AS-SINA, meaning wharf or workshop. It was Venice's shipyard, the Republic's chief industry, upon which its wealth + power had been built + depended, + included a foundry for making guns, cannons, swords etc. It was founded in 1104 + enlarged over the centuries, at times employing 16,000 workers. Once the world's greatest ship-yard, it introduced assembly-line production + adopted a uniform system of measurement that standardized ships' individual parts, making it easier to build, repair + maintain them. Masts, oars, sails, pulleys, bows + arrows, ropes —everything ships needed was produced within the high brick walls surrounding the Arsenale. Its activity was classified + protected from espionage; thus, it was unlawful to climb the high tower of the nearby church of San Francesco della Vigna which affords a view of it + foreigners were prohibited from going to the top of the Campanile di San Marco for similar reasons. During WWI, Italy's Adriatic fleet was kept there but the Arsenale was greatly dismantled towards the end of that war to keep it from falling into enemy hands. Projects for a future use are often proposed but its fate remains uncertain.

Sally Spector

Onion CIPOLLA segola fam. Liliaceae, Allium cepa

The Latin word UNIO, meaning oneness or unity, which is the origin of the word union, also gave birth to the word onion —OIGNON in French— but for the ancient Romans this plant was CEPA, a word of unknown origin from which the Italian CIPOLLA and the Venetian SEGOLA both derive. Like their close relatives, garlics and leeks, onions are native to Western and Central Asia; from Assyria and Babylonia they spread to Egypt, then into Greece and Italy and the Mediterranean and from there, through the rest of Europe. They have been cultivated for thousands of years and for the ancient Egyptians, onions were sacred. The ancient Romans, who used other bulbs, such as the gladiolus and hyacinth, in their cuisine considered the onion a poor person's food, probably because of the strong odor it leaves on the breath when eaten raw but they did recognize its medicinal properties: they used onions to expell intestinal worms and parasites and as an external antiseptic but they were most important as a prevention against scurvey due to their Vitamin C content. Thus soldiers, and especially sailors, of the Roman Empire ate lots of them, as did seamen of the Venetian Republic; in fact, one of Venice's oldest and most traditional dishes, called SARDELE IN SAOR (p.137), contains a great deal of onions and was a common food on board ship. Their use as a flavoring or condiment, in addition to being a food, began when the Eastern spice trade started to decline in the late 1600's and grew steadily from then on The numerous varieties of onions available today are distinguished according to: the form of their bulb - round, disk-shaped, pear-shaped or oblong; the color of their external skin — white, yellow, pink or red ; their taste —from very sweet to sharp and hot— and the season they are harvested in. Venetians normally use common yellow or white onions for the SOFFRITTO; a type of round white onion called AGOSTANA DI CHIOGGIA, grown in the lagoon, is particularly prized. These members of the lily family are always cooked very gently for Venetian dishes, never 'til dark or blackened which makes them too strong tasting.

Garlic   AGLIO   agio   fam. Liliaceae, Allium sativum

Garlic is native to the Middle East and the Mediterranean area though today it grows throughout the Northern Hemisphere; it does not like humid climates nor does it grow in forests. The Italian word AGLIO and the Venetian AGIO come from the Latin ALLIU while two Old English words give us garlic: GAR, meaning spear, refers to its pointed leaves and/or its pungent taste and LEAC, meaning leek. During the Roman Empire it was eaten in great quantities, with onions, by soldiers, oarsmen and those who did heavy physical work. Garlic was generally associated with poor people but nonetheless since antiquity, it was believed to have powerful healing properties and for centuries continued to be used as an antidote for poison as well as a cure for assorted pains and illnesses, which is why it was known as "poor man's treacle" (from THERION and THERIAKE in Greek, meaning "wild beast" and "remedy for bites" and THERIACA in Latin, meaning "antidote for poison"). Venetians, and Italians in general, use much less of this bulbous plant than is popularly imagined. Many of the garlic presses on the market are made in Italy but few people here use one: they peel the clove and chop it on a cutting board, often squashing it first by pressing on it with the flat side of a wide knife blade. It is sometimes peeled and left whole, gently heated in oil and then removed, cooked just enough to give food a hint of its flavor.

Carrot   CAROTA   carota   fam. Umbelliferae, Daucus carota

This edible root, native to Europe, is an important food for both humans and domestic animals today but the ancient Greeks used it for medicinal purposes: their word KAROTON is the source for its name in Latin, Italian, English and other languages. In Europe, serious cultivation of the carrot started around 1300 but was not widespread until the late 1600's. The once great diversity among carrots was much reduced in the 1700's when the Low Countries experimented with breeding them and created the three main types that those cultivated today derive from, distinguished by their

color, length (short, medium or long) and maturation period. In addition to the familiar orange carrot there are also white and yellow ones, used for fodder: the yellow one is much sweeter than the orange but when cooked it gives food a strange brown color

thought rather unappetizing and is thus avoided in the kitchen. The Veneto is among Italy's major carrot producers and the soil around Chioggia is particularly favorable for it.

Celery SEDANO seano fam. Umbelliferae, Apium graveolens

The Greeks called this plant SELINON from which its name in Latin, Italian and English all derive. Essential in some DESFRITI, such as MINESTRA DE POMODORO (p. 50), for its subtle but distinctive taste, it is optional in others, where its inclusion depends on personal preference or family tradition. Instead of an entire bunch, one usually buys just a few stalks here, called GAMBI, meaning stems or stalks (legs are GAMBE), and they come white or green. The white variety, more tender and delicate tasting, is eaten raw and in milder dishes; the green one has a thicker, tougher stalk and a stronger taste and is used for SOFFRITTI, stewing and soups. I have never been a great lover of celery, and it does seem absurd to rave about it, but the lagoon's gardens produce an incredibly delicious example of this vegetable.

GOTHIC WINDOWS Venetian arches were systematically separated into categories by the English writer & critic, John Ruskin (1819-1900), which he called "orders". According to him, these three-lobed pointed arches belong to the 4th order, common in Venetian architecture from the late 1200's to about 1450.

Parsley   PREZZEMOLO parsemolo   fam. Umbelliferae, Petroselinum hortense

While this aromatic plant is native to the Mediterranean area and grows wild in southern Europe, it adapts to a wide range of climatic conditions, from dry to damp and from hot to cold. In fact, its name derives from the Greek word PETROSELINON, meaning "celery that grows out of the stones". By the 16th century it was widespread throughout western Europe and England and is now cultivated in temperate areas all over the world. The ancient Greeks and Romans used it for medicinal purposes: as an emmenagogue, because it was thought to provoke menstruation, and as a diuretic; later it was used to relieve obstructions of the liver and spleen and for circulatory and kidney problems. While official medicine still recognizes it as a possible remedy for inflamation of the urinary tract, its principal use today is in the kitchen. There are two main types of parsley — flat-leafed and curly-leafed. The flat-leafed, also called Italian or Neapolitan parsley, is used in the Mediterranean world; it has more flavor than the curly one commonly used in North America and England where it is more a garnish than a taste. The flat-leafed is much preferred, and recommended whenever possible, although both are rich in vitamins and also contain calcium. In Venice, as everywhere in Italy, parsley is sold loose in the markets, not in pre-packaged bunches, and one buys as much as desired; Venetians do not use dried parsley but some people keep it in the freezer — it is sold frozen, already minced, in little boxes, which can be useful in emergencies. A crescent-shaped cutter, or MEZZA-LUNA, is considered the best implement for mincing parsley; for more coarse chopping, the leaves can be put in a small glass and snipped inside it with a scissor.

Italians use the phrase "ESSERE COME IL PREZZEMOLO" "to be like parsley" to describe a person or thing that goes everywhere which, depending on the context can be positive, negative or, occasionally, neutral.

RIO TERA DEI BIRI O DEL PARSEMOLO

The above street sign translates as: FILLED-IN CANAL of the BIRI or of PARSLEY. It is believed that BIRI derives from BIERUM, meaning a canal whose water provided energy for turning mills. Why it was also called "OR PARSLEY" is not documented. This RIO TERÀ is near the Church of San Cancian in Cannaregio.

Pancetta   panceta

PANCIA is belly, paunch or stomach in Italian and PANCETTA is the diminutive form. "Little belly" is thus the literal translation of the Italian term for salted, unsmoked ham, cut from the pig's stomach: it is its abdominal fat —from which bacon also comes— streaked with meat, and is conserved by first salting it in brine for from 48 to 72 hours, after which it is completely covered with salt and left to sit for eight days. It is then ready to be consumed as PANCETTA and keeps for a fairly long time if stored in a cool, dark place. Once the pork has undergone the salting process it can be seasoned with spices or herbs, formed into a cylindrical shape and left out to dry in the air to become salami. It can also be smoked or made into bacon, which the Italians call SPECK, from the German word for lard, but this is done only in the northern regions of Trentino and Alto Adige, which were once part of Austria. PANCETTA comes in two forms —cylindrical or a rectangular slab: the round one is more mild and used in Venetian cooking while the rectangular one is more common in central and southern Italy. Some Venetian butchers offer two varieties of the round PANCETTA: one for cooking and one for making sandwiches. For the DESFRITO, the PANCETA is cut in a single slice and then chopped at home according to the requirements of the particular recipe.

Broth   BRODO   brodo

It may surprise people, as it did me, to learn that even excellent, serious cooks in Venice use bouillon cubes for broth when making RISOTTI and MINESTRE, although everyone admits that homemade is usually best. The water used for boiling fish normally becomes the broth for sea-food RISOTTI, and that made from vegetable stems or pea pods is quite easy to prepare, but the use of bouillon cubes is not considered to be a limiting factor: Italian, and European, cubes are extremely good. Some people always use them and some

AMPHORA from well-head dated 14th-15th century in Corte de la Madonna near Campo Santa Margherita, Dorsoduro

people use them for everyday cooking and make broth for company and special occasions, but sometimes just plain water is preferred because it is felt the BRODO overpowers the taste of the other ingredients; unlike those cuisines in which a rich stock and sauce are fundamental, the quality and savor of Venetian rice dishes depend almost entirely on the delicacy of the DESFRITO. Venetians usually put the dry cube in with the vegetables of the DESFRITO, which dissolves as they release their water content, and then add hot water when boiling the rice. If the prescribed amount of liquid has been used up and the rice still seems too crunchy, hot water is added to finish its cooking.

MAGAZZINO or MAGAZEN shed-like store-room near the Rialto Market in Campo Rialto Novo, San Polo

Salli Spector

Part of most Venetian buildings, many of these ground floor MAGAZENI are no longer used for storage.

Butter BURRO butiro

The roots of the word butter lie in the Greek and Latin BUTIROM and in the Medieval French BURE. In Italy, during the Middle Ages the ancient term -BUTIROM- was predominant; in different places it varied and thus butter was called BUTIRO, BUTIRRO, BUTIERO, BUTERIUS, BOTURO, BOTIRO or BITURRO but eventually the French word BURRE prevailed and became BURRO in Italian. Venetians, however, still say BUTIRO. Butter's history dates to the remote past. Thousands of years ago shepherds of the ancient Middle East churned milk inside of goatskin bags, producing a butter more liquidy than today's, which was probably more like buttermilk, and it is thought that East Indians were making it as long ago as 1,500 B.C. For centuries, its therapeutic uses, as an ointment for treating skin diseases and eye ailments, were much more important than its nutritive ones. It served as a pomade for grooming hair in ancient Rome, where it was considered to be a food only for barbarians, such as the Celts and Germanic peoples from the north. In fact, Julius Cesar wrote that he ate butter for the first time in Milan, in 55 B.C., where it was served on asparagus: he found it surprising and unappetizing. Later, in northern Europe, where oil was more scarce than butter, it was used as a lubricant, for greasing ships' ropes and lighting lamps.

Butter is the mixture of fat globules, air bubbles and water droplets contained in the oily part of cow's milk which, due to gravity, rises to the top of this liquid. Since it is very perishable and spoils if exposed to air and light, it did not lend itself to the trade and transport conditions of the past, as did olive oil, although there was some commerce in rancid butter. Its production remained very local —virtually on a family scale— until the second half of the 1800's when the Industrial Revolution was underway: by means of centrifugal force, the fatty cream was skimmed off milk mechanically, left to ferment and then beaten or churned into butter, thus modernizing a process that had always been extremely long and laborious.

Sometimes butter is salted to conserve it and this is very common in North America and England. In Italy, however, where traditionally things have been consumed fresh, unsalted butter is used. Until a few years ago, it was still possible to buy a tiny piece of fresh, unpackaged butter but due to industrial production and modern hygienic regulations this can no longer be done. Italians, and Mediterranean people in general, have always preferred vegetable fat to animal fat, thus olive oil instead of butter or lard, and this is probably what most differentiates the cuisine of southern Europe from northern Europe. Venetian cooking uses very little butter; some people never put it in their DESFRITI and use only olive oil, while others occasionally add it to the oil, but it is essential for making sweets. Margarine is now available although I know no one who uses it and most people here have probably never eaten it.

AMPHORA
from well-
head, dated
14th-15th cent.
in Campiello
del Pestrin near
Palazzo Widmann,
Cannaregio

CALLE & PONTE DEL PESTRIN
near Campo Santo Stefano, San Marco

The word PESTRIN comes from the Latin word PESTRINUM, which was the place where the ancient Romans ground grain, originally by hand with a mortar & pestle; subsequently PESTRINUM referred to the mill where grinding was done between heavy stones turned by animals —usually horses— or by slaves. Venetians adopted the word PESTRIN for their city's mills that ground grain into flour & flax seeds into oil & since these mills were usually turned by cows, the word became associated with these bovines & with dairy products. It was applied to milk sellers, called PESTRINERI, as well as to the places where butter & cheese were made. Historical documents show that government officials would often surprise PESTRINERI with unannounced inspections of their PESTRIN to ascertain that the cows were not fed the residue of the ground flax seeds considered harmful for the animals & also for the people who ate the butter & cheese made from their milk. The most common cheeses produced were RICOTTA & FIOR DI LATTE, or "flowers of milk" similar to a very soft cream cheese. The word FIOR —from FIORE, meaning flower— is used to indicate the best or purest part of something: FIOR DI FARINA is the finest flour, FIOR DI LATTE is the cream from milk.

CALLE DEL
PESTRIN

Oil   OLIO   ogio

The olive tree is the symbol of the Mediterranean world. It is native to the Middle East and the ancient Phoenicians, who lived in what is now Syria and Lebanon, may have been the first people to recognize its various uses. They exported olive oil to Egypt and introduced this plant into Greece, where it enjoys its most favorable climatic conditions. Today it grows in many temperate zones in the northern hemisphere: the northernmost point at which olives grow - 45°- marks the upper limit of the so-called Mediterranean climate and its southern boundary - 30°- lies where the great groves of palm trees begin. Venice is situated midway between the 45th and 46th parallel north, thus barely outside the "olive area." No other plant is imbued with as much significance as this one, recognized throughout the Western World as a symbol of Peace, Wisdom, Strength, Joy and Fertility. Called the "King of Trees", it grows quite slowly, taking from thirty to forty years to become fruitful, but continues to bear olives for hundreds of years. Because even a chopped-off stump regenerates, it was revered as a sacred plant in ancient Greece where it was protected by officials who put anyone who cut down an olive tree in prison.

Today olive oil is used mostly for cooking but it had several functions in the past, from the spiritual to the mundane. In religious rituals it served for offerings and to consecrate priests and sacred objects; it was also used to anoint athletes and sick people, for cosmetics, as cooking fat and for illumination. In addition, there was a thriving trade based on oil all over the Mediterranean, as the countless ancient ceramic amphoras found in this area demonstrate. During the Middle Ages it found new uses: in the 1300's Venetians made soap with olive oil imported from Puglia, in southern Italy, which made a harder, whiter, better smelling product than the usual

AMPHORA of the type produced in Puglia from early 7th to 14th cent., used for exporting olive oil. This type of amphora was very present throughout the lagoon area.

tallow soap and it became almost a luxury item. Venetian merchants also derived great profits from the re-exportation of olive oil, from Venice to northern Europe, where it was used predominantly as a lubricant in the thriving textile industry there. It continued to be one of Venice's most important commodities during the 16th and 17th centuries and even in the 1770's, more than half of the oil imported here was re-exported by Venetian middlemen.

Olive trees are not part of the Venetian landscape today, but place names in the lagoon show that they were once present. An area called Valle Olivara or Olivari, in the north lagoon, appears on maps from as early as the 10th century and strongly suggests the cultivation of olives; while the name has remained (VALLE, or valley, refers to places in the lagoon that are deeper than average and used for the breeding and raising of fish), the trees have disappeared, but there are still a few in this zone, on the island of Torcello, and historical documents show that during the Middle Ages the inhabitants of this and neighboring islands had to pay their rent in olive oil.

In addition, the island of San Pietro di Castello, at the easternmost edge of Venice, was originally called Olivolo, thought to be due to the presence of olives, of which all traces have disappeared. Thus, Venetians produced some oil but most of their needs were filled with imports from Puglia, Romania and the Eastern Mediterranean, especially from the Peloponnesus and from the island of Crete.

AMPHORA
from well-head dated 14th-15th cent. in Campiello Santa Marina, off Campo San Marina, Castello

Numerous place names in Venice reflect the once very significant role that olive oil had in the city's economic activity: PONTE DE L'OGIO, FONDAMENTA DE L'OGIO, CALLE DE L'OGIO and CORTE DE L'OGIO all indicate bridges, streets and courtyards where it was unloaded, stored and sold. Its value is also seen its frequent appearance in old Venetian wills and testaments as a possession bequeathed to survivors.

Two of Venice's oldest guilds, founded in the 1200's, had to do with oil and the regulations of its commerce: the SAGOMADORI measured it and the TERNIERI sold it. The SAGOMADORI, from the Greek word SACOMA, meaning "correct measure", controlled and measured the barrels that oil was stored in, as well as the containers for honey, using instruments produced by and belonging to the State. The word TERNIER derives from the Latin TERNI, meaning "three of something"; as early as the 12th century Venice had established a body of officers in charge of collecting duties on all types of alimentary products and since this responsibility was originally shared by three magistrates, it was called the TERNARIA. Both the taxes and the warehouses that stored food were also called TERNARIA, as were the sellers of oil, honey and fatty pork products but the word, which in the early 1800's was considered an antique term and was rarely used, has completely disappeared from the Venetian dialect of today. To protect the public from fraud and to maintain quality, it was unlawful to mix oil from Puglia with that from central Italy and label it as "PUGLIESE," but oil from Rumania could be mixed with Puglia's and sold under either name.

Olive trees grow almost everywhere in Italy —only the most northern regions are excluded— and it is the world's major producer of olive oil, followed by Spain and Greece. It is estimated that there are some one hundred million olive trees in Italy, or almost two per person. These trees bear many different types of olives and consequently, their oil varies, not only from one region to another but sometimes even within the same region: there are more than 30 types just within Sicily. Other factors contributing to these variations are differences in soil composition, the water of their environment and the agricultural techniques used in cultivating them. Olive trees require much care and attention and need ample growing space: the distance between trees ranges from three to seven meters. The way olives are harvested is also important, whether picked by hand, gently raked off their branches and caught by suspended nets, or shaken so as to fall to the ground. In addition, their state of ripeness, how they are transported from the fields to the olive press —if, for example, they are bruised in the process— and the methods of extracting their oil all effect the type and quality of oil produced. The pressing of olives to make oil, originally done with heavy stones, remained virtually unchanged from antiquity until the 1600's when the screw press began to be used; the hydraulic press modernized this process in the 1700's and is still used today.

Extra-virgin is the uncontested "King" of Italian olive oil and to merit this name it must have less than one percent acidity. It is more expensive than the other qualities of olive oil but it is the purest — it contains no chemicals or additives — and the most healthy and digestible: it even helps to digest other fats. Its superiority also means that it renders more and thus it can be used in smaller quantities than ordinary types. Italians believe that the oil of a particular region is the one best suited to that local cuisine: thus, Tuscan oil for typically Tuscan dishes, Ligurian oil for the cooking of Liguria, etc. The oil produced in the Veneto, of which the supply is very limited, comes from the shores of Lake Garda, far enough away from Venice and with a cuisine different enough from this city's to leave Venetians free to choose whichever olive oil they like best, although northern Italians tend to prefer lighter oil than do people in central and southern Italy. While Venetians normally use vegetable seed oil to fry fish and for deep-frying, they use olive oil for everything else.

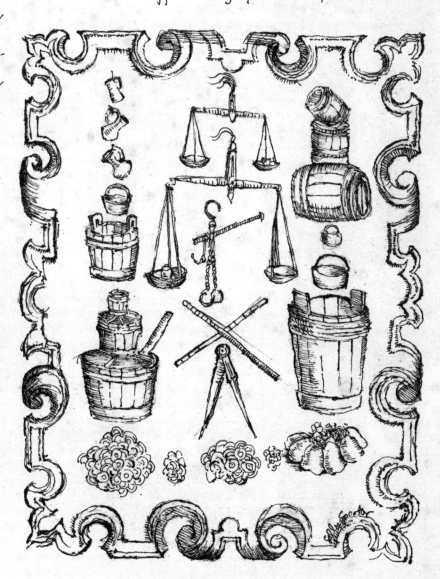

INSTRUMENTS & CONTAINERS

for MEASURING from woodcut in TARIFFA PERPETUA by the 16th cent. Venetian Giovanni Mariani. He worked in the CAMERA DEGL' PRESTITI, or Board of Loans; his writings deal with prices & weights & their relative amounts in foreign equivalents, useful for international trade as well as within Italy's borders. TARIFFA PERPETUA, first printed in 1575 in Venice by Francesco Rampazetto, is like a primitive pocket calculator: it measures 17 x 8 x 4.5 cm. (6½ x 3¼ x 1¾ in.), filled with tables for converting MONEDA VENEZIANA (Venetian money) into other values. From the edition printed in 1591 by Giovanni Antonio Rampazetto. (Marciana Library)

SOTOPORT
DE LE COLON

Sally Spector

The FONDAMENTA & SOTOPORTEGO
of the "columns", in
Cannaregio, is around the
corner from what was once a warehouse
for oil, as indicated by the CALLE & CORTE
DE L'OGIO nearby, strategically located
on an important water way: the
canal —RIO DE LA MADALENA— was,
& still is, a link from the Grand
Canal to the north lagoon
towards Murano
& Burano.

MINESTRA DI POMODORO   RICE & TOMATO SOUP

Most Venetians over the age of 50, as well ISOLANI, or "islanders" as the natives of the lagoon's islands are called, remember eating this dish when they were young. As already described, the Venetian MINESTRA is a sort of rice-soup, of a more humble character than the RISOTTO and more economical: it uses RISO COMUNE, the least expensive type of rice and the amount is about half that required for the RISOTTO — 1½ oz. rice per person for MINESTRE, 3-3¾ oz. for RISOTTI. Like much simple, peasant food, it is unpretentious and delicious.

~ 4 SERVINGS ~

2 TB. OLIVE OIL

1 medium ONION } finely
1   "   CARROT } chopped
1 stalk CELERY

sprig of fresh ROSEMARY

1 QT. hot BROTH*

3 fresh peeled, chopped
            OR
2 cups canned TOMATOES

6 OZ. RICE "COMUNE"

SALT & PEPPER

freshly grated PARMESAN CHEESE

* if using BOUILLON, keep the CUBE & hot WATER separate

If there is leftover MINESTRA it will turn into PAPPA, or baby food, which is also the word for overcooked, mushy rice & PASTA. It can be 'recycled' in a blender to become a creamy version of this dish.

1) Put the OIL, ONION, CARROT, CELERY & ROSEMARY in a pot. If using BOUILLON for the BROTH, put the dry cube in with the vegetables. Cook slowly, covered, about 20 minutes 'til they are wilted & the CARROT is soft. As they release their water content, the BOUILLON dissolves. Stir occasionally.

2) Add the TOMATOES, squashing them in with the other ingredients. Cook uncovered until the liquid has evaporated.

3) Add the RICE, stirring it well in with the vegetables.

4) Raise the heat to medium & add about ¾ of the BROTH or WATER at once. The mixture should boil gently, uncovered, about 15 minutes. Stir occasionally.

5) Taste the RICE. If it is still too crunchy, continue cooking a bit longer. Season with SALT & PEPPER. Add the rest of the hot BROTH or WATER. Serve with PARMESAN CHEESE.

Until fairly recently there was much poverty in the Veneto — having enough to eat was a continual problem — & the winters are cold & damp. This humble MINESTRA "TI INCOCONA" as the Venetians say, meaning it "fills you up", "stuffs your stomach", which can be a very pleasing sensation, greatly valued in the past.

MINESTRA DE VERZE   RICE & CABBAGE SOUP

Like the MINESTRA DI POMODORO, this dish was once very popular in Venice. Cabbage is among the "oldest" produce of the lagoon and has been cultivated in this area for centuries; many of the lagoon's islands were occupied by religious institutions, especially Benedictine and Augustinian monasteries and convents and this was one of the most common vegetables grown in their gardens. Since it is picked all year long, it was a very useful food, particularly in winter when few fresh vegetables were available.

~ 4 SERVINGS ~

1 medium CABBAGE, very thinly sliced,✳ rinsed & drained

1 small ONION, finely chopped

1 TB. each, BUTTER & OIL

SALT & PEPPER

1 QT. hot BROTH ▶

6 OZ. RICE "COMUNE"

2 TB. minced fresh PARSLEY

1) Cook the ONION in the BUTTER & OIL very slowly until soft. It must not burn.

2) Add the CABBAGE with a bit of SALT & PEPPER. Raise the heat a bit & stir until it begins to wither.

3) Lower the heat. If using BOUILLON for the BROTH, add the dry CUBE, cover & cook very slowly about 40 minutes. Stir occasionally. The CABBAGE should become very tender.

4) Proceed according to Steps 3, 4 & 5 of the recipe for MINESTRA DI POMODORO p. 50; instead of PARMESAN, add the PARSLEY.

✳ Venetians do not grate CABBAGE, they slice it. Italian graters are designed for grating PARMESAN CHEESE but multi-purpose ones are now available. Sliced cabbage is more pleasing than grated for this dish.

▶ if using BOUILLON, keep the CUBE & hot WATER separate

Although cabbage seems a rather uncomplicated vegetable, calling it by its right name in Venice can be confusing & almost comical. In Italy, different terms are used in different places for certain foods & what is CAVOLO or cabbage, in one place may be CAVOLFIORE, or cauliflower in another. Generally speaking, in Venice, smooth cabbage is CAPPUCCIO, meaning 'hood', VERZA has wavy or curly leaves & CAVOLO may be one or the other.

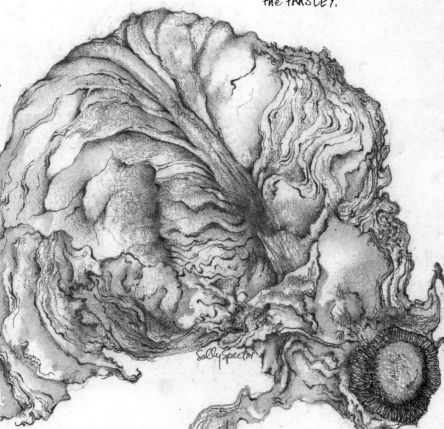

sallySpector

RISO co'l LATE   RICE with MILK

This was once a very common dish in Venice and many people have pleasant memories of it since it recalls their childhood. It was usually given to youngsters but was also highly recommended for those with delicate stomachs. Sometimes raisins, soaked first in tepid water to swell them up a bit, and pine nuts were added, signs of Venice's commerce with the Eastern Mediterranean. Mattioli (p.21) wrote that cooking rice in milk not only made it easier to digest but also rendered it more delicious and that the addition of sugar and cinnamon would increase virility.

~4 SERVINGS~

2 QT. MILK — whole or skim or a combination of both

13 OZ. RICE "FINO" or "SUPER-FINO"

OPTIONAL INGREDIENTS
{ SALT, BUTTER,
freshly grated PARMESAN CHEESE }
OR
{ 2 TB. RAISINS
"   "   PINE NUTS }

1) Bring the MILK to the boiling point over medium heat. Do not let it reach a full boil.

2) Add the RICE & cook, simmering, for about 18 minutes. Do not cover & stir often to keep the RICE from sticking to the bottom of the pot. If the RICE is still too crunchy after 18 minutes, continue its cooking & test for desired firmness.

3) Serve as is or with OPTIONAL INGREDIENTS

The illustration on the following page is copied from an engraving by Gaetano Zompini (1700-1778). Born in nearby Treviso, Zompini worked as a painter but is most famous for a series of engravings he did from 1746-1754, known as "Le arti che vanno per via nella città di Venezia", or "The Street Vendors of Venice". These sixty prints depict the work of everyday life: peddlers selling vegetables, fish, cookies, pots, rags, brooms, rat poison, worn shoes, old iron, the chimney sweep, the knife sharpener...etc.

Each print is accompanied by a brief verse in Venetian about the subject. Zompini was encouraged & supported in this endeavor by the famous art collector, Anton Maria Zanetti, (1706-1778), a leading figure in the musical, literary & artistic life of the 18th century; for many years he was curator of the marciana Library.

Copied from a set of original engravings in the Library of the Fondazione Querini-Stampalia.

"Per barca tanto late avemo usanza
Portar zo da Campalto, e Botenigo;
Che in tuta la Citae ghe n'è abondanza."

(By boat so much milk we bring
From Campalto and Botenigo
That the city has it in abundance.)

Products such as milk, cheese, chickens & eggs came from the mainland where there were farms (today Campalto is a 'suburb' of Venice) & were normally brought by women who rowed across the lagoon to sell these goods in the city. Women likewise brought fruit & vegetables from the gardens of Chioggia & Sant'Erasmo (p.148) where they did much of the farming since men were occupied with fishing.

RISI E BISI   RICE & PEAS

When asked to name their city's most famous dish, most Venetians will say, RISI E BISI — BISI are peas in Venetian, PISELLI in Italian. While it is extremely good, its fame is also greatly due to its historic significance for it was the official dish served to the Doge on the 25th of April, the feast day of St. Mark, Venice's patron saint; it was one of the Republic's most important holidays, celebrated with a solemn procession in Piazza San Marco. On that day, the most beautiful peas in the orchards of the lagoon were gathered for the Doge's portion and the onion for the DESFRITO had to be freshly picked at the same time. If the winter had been very long or cold and the peas were not ripe yet, they were brought from elsewhere: those from Genoa were especially prized. Foreign ambassadors, royalty and other illustrious visitors in Venice during the pea season were always served RISI e BISI. The Doge is no more, but when the peas in the lagoon are ripe, Venetians still make this dish.

RISI E BISI is somewhere between a MINESTRA and a RISOTTO... most people eat it with a spoon. The restaurant version is usually not as liquidy as the traditional homemade one. RISI E BISI should be "ALL'ONDA", or "with waves"; this Venetian phrase means that the rice has enough broth so that if you tip your bowl, the liquid moves enough to make a tiny wave.

～ 4 SERVINGS ～

2 TB. OLIVE OIL

5 TB. BUTTER

1 small ONION, finely chopped

2 LB fresh or 8 OZ. frozen PEAS

pinch of SUGAR

1 1/2 QT. hot BROTH

10 OZ. RICE "FINO" or "SUPER-FINO"

SALT & PEPPER

2-3 TB. minced fresh PARSLEY

freshly grated PARMESAN CHEESE

According to Venetian legend there was supposed to be one PEA for every grain of RICE in the Doge's bowl of RISI E BISI.

RISI E BISI is best made with tiny fresh PEAS whose PODS are boiled to make the BROTH but many people use frozen ones & make the BROTH with BOUILLON.

1) Shell the PEAS. Rinse the PODS & put them in 2 QT. salted WATER or put in a BOUILLON CUBE & no SALT. Boil very slowly for one hour, half-covered.

2) Strain the BROTH. Press the liquid out of the PODS & discard them. If using BOUILLON for the liquid, prepare 1½ QT. of it.

3) Put the ONION, OIL & 2½ TB. BUTTER in a pot. Cook gently until golden.

4) Add the PEAS with a pinch of SUGAR & a bit of BROTH. Cook gently, stirring occasionally, until they soften. (add frozen peas straight from the freezer, without defrosting)

5) When the liquid has evaporated & the mixture is "dry", add the RICE. Raise the heat & mix the RICE in quickly with the other ingredients.

6) Pour in a ladel of hot BROTH; the mixture should be boiling. Stir constantly, adding a ladel of BROTH when the liquid has reduced, making sure that the RICE never sticks to the pot. After about 18 minutes the RICE should be done; taste to check & if it is still too crunchy, continue cooking another minute or two.

7) Turn off heat. Taste for SALT & PEPPER. Add a ladel of BROTH, the remaining BUTTER & the PARSLEY but do not mix them in. Cover the pot & leave on the extinguished burner for 2-3 minutes, then gently stir all of the ingredients together.

8) Serve immediately with freshly grated PARMESAN CHEESE.

LION OF SAN MARCO from the Porta della Carta, or "Door of the Paper," the main entrance into the public part of Palazzo Ducale in Piazza San Marco. The name refers to the State Archives & the Scribes who wrote petitions & official papers near to it. Begun in 1438, the Door is the work of Giovanni & Bartolomeo Bon. The original statues of the Lion & the Doge Francesco Foscari (1423-1457) who kneels at its feet were destroyed in 1797 & replaced in 1885 by copies made by the Venetian sculptor Luigi Ferrari (1810-1894), who followed their dimensions & positions as closely as possible.

The winged lion is virtually synonymous for Venice. It is one of the four mysterious beings that the Apostle John described in his writing known as the Revelations or Apocalypse, which are very similar to the ones that appeared in the vision of the prophet Ezekiel. Later, in the 4th century, St. Jerome interpreted the images of these beings and he ascribed them to the four Evangelists. The lion became Mark's attribute because his Gospel emphasizes Christ's regality and the lion was a symbol of royalty. But, of greater significance for Venetians, Mark had personal ties with the lagoon for he had come here to preach and to found the Patriarchate of Acquileia, 100 kms. east of Venice. Legend says that after doing this, a storm kept his boat from returning to Rome and was washed on the mud flats of the present Rialto area where he fell asleep and dreamed that an angel said to him "PAX TIBI MARCE", or "Peace to you, Mark", and told him one day his body would return to rest where he was and a great city would be built to house his remains. He was buried in Alexandria, Egypt and it is said that two Venetian merchants secretly brought his body to Venice in 828, after which he replaced Theodore as the city's patron saint: the winged lion became its emblem and PAX TIBI MARCE its motto. Probably no other religious symbol has been so closely identified with a temporal reality as Mark's winged lion for it represented the government and State of Venice as well as its spiritual essence. Thus, the Venetians' reverence for Mark is not limited to the sacred; his lion is the symbol of their city and "VIVA SAN MARCO" is the cry of Venetian patriots.

The lion is usually shown standing on three legs while the fourth holds a book —an open book indicates a time of peace, a closed book means a time of war— or as a portrait, with its wings spread in a circular frame around it. The portrait is known as "IL LEONE IN MOLECA" for its resemblance to the lagoon's tiny crabs, or MOLECHE, during the brief period when they shed their hard shell and become soft-shelled, which makes them a famous Venetian gastronomic treat. (p.142) The lion here is on a silver coin minted by Venice's 92nd Doge, Giovanni Bembo (1615-1618) and was worth 140 SOLDI or 7 LIRE VENETE. The gold and silver coins minted by the Venetian Republic were recognized almost everywhere.

WATER-DOOR, or PORTA DA ACQUA, in the Venetian-Byzantine style, 13th cent., on the Rio della Pietà, Castello

RISI e PATATE
~ 4 SERVINGS ~
RICE with POTATOES

2 TB. OLIVE OIL
1 TB. BUTTER

1 small ONION, finely chopped

⟨OPTIONAL: 2 OZ. PANCETTA, finely chopped⟩

4 medium POTATOES - peeled & cut into small pieces

1 QT. hot BROTH✱ or WATER

13 OZ. RICE "FINO" or "SUPER-FINO"

SALT & PEPPER

2 TB. minced fresh PARSLEY

freshly grated PARMESAN CHEESE

✱ if using BOUILLON, keep the CUBE & WATER separate

1) Cook the ONION & optional PANCETTA in the OIL & BUTTER over low heat until the ONION is tender & transparent. It should not brown.

2) Add the POTATOES & a bit of BROTH or the dry BOUILLON CUBE & a bit of hot WATER. Cook them, stirring constantly —they tend to stick to the pot but should not— for 10-15 minutes.

3) Raise the heat & add the RICE, mixing it quickly in with the other ingredients.

4) Add a ladel of BROTH or WATER. The mixture should be boiling. Stir constantly, adding a ladel of hot BROTH when the liquid has reduced, making sure the RICE & POTATOES do not stick to the pot.

5) After about 18 minutes the RICE should be done. Taste for SALT & PEPPER & stir in the PARSLEY.

6) Turn off heat. Cover the pot & leave it on the extinguished burner for 2 minutes. Serve immediately with PARMESAN CHEESE.

RISI e PATATE is not as common today as it once was, perhaps because its contents seem so simple, so ordinary, but it is both unusual & delicious. Its secret lies in the texture & consistency of the ingredients: the POTATOES should combine with the RICE without becoming mushy & provide a pleasing contrast to the slight "bite" of the RICE....
...other recipes using POTATOES are on pages 86 + 89.

Sally Spector

Potato   PATATA patata   fam Solanaceae, Solanum tuberosum

The potato originated in Chile. It was not only an important food for South American Indians but archaeological evidence in the form of clay pottery and sculpture shows that they attributed it with supernatural powers and used it in their magic rituals. Europeans, however, felt quite differently about this tuber: explorers who brought potatoes back to Spain from the New World in the early 1500's considered them suitable only for cattle fodder. In spite of this attitude, the Venetian humanist, Andrea Navagero (1483-1529), was willing to try them. While in Spain from 1524-1528 as a representative of the Venetian Republic, he described this strange food in a letter to his friend Giovanni Battista Ramusio (1485-1557) the great geographer and cartographer:

"Io ho veduto molte cose dell'India ed io ho avute di quelle radici che chiamano batatas e le ho mangiate: sono di sapor di castagne."

(I have seen many things from India and I have had some of those roots called batatas and I ate them: they taste like chestnuts.)

It is not clear exactly how the potato got to Italy. It is thought that Carmelite monks brought it from Spain or Portugal towards the end of the 1500's but this plant was viewed with disdain, seen as not fit for humans except in periods of famine when there was nothing else to eat. Its rather unattractive physical appearance limited its appeal and the fact that it grew underground, in the dark, made it suspect...vestiges of the medieval concept of the hierarchy of foods in which plants, and especially tubers, occupied the lowest order of the cosmos, being farthest from heaven. Terrestrial animals and fish were in the middle while birds, because they are closest to the celestial sphere, were most prized and thus were reserved for the nobel, wealthy and otherwise privileged.

The potato continued to be rejected, even by poor hungry peasants, until the 1700's when European agronomists began to find it interesting because of its ability to adapt to a variety of growing conditions, its resistence to cold and its extremely high productivity: it thrives at elevations of 5,000 meters (15,000 feet!) and can withstand frost. They wrote treatises and books to encourage the acceptance of the potato as a source of food for people even in times of plenty; probably its best known champion was the French agronomist-economist-pharmacist, Antoine-Augustin Parmentier (1738-1813), whose work urging its cultivation was published in 1773 but, six years earlier, a citizen of the Venetian Republic had already printed a work on this subject. Antonio Zanon (1696-1770), from Udine in the Friuli region, under Venetian domain, was an agronomist-economist; his book Della coltivazione e dell'uso delle patate e d'altre piante comestibili was published in Venice in 1767 (On the cultivation and use of potatoes and other comestible plants), two years after his book entitled Dell'agricoltura dell'arti e del commercio, in quanto unite contribuiscono alla felicità degli stati (On Agriculture, the trades and commerce which, when united, contribute to the happiness of countries), both titles indicative of his auspicious, enlightened vision of agriculture.

By the late 1700's Italian peasants were eating potatoes although they were far more popular in northern Europe. In fact, it was the Austrians who, bringing their eating habits with them when they occupied Venice from 1798 to 1806 and again from 1814 to 1866, were largely responsible for its increased acceptance here. But, the credit for the potato's entry into Italian cooking goes to Pellegrino Artusi (1820-1911). His book, La Scienza in cucina e l'Arte di mangiar bene - Manuale pratico per le famiglie (Science in the kitchen and the art of eating well - A practical manual for families), consisting of 475 recipes, was first published at his own expense in 1891, reprinted at least 111 times and remains a classic. This book proposed a "standardized" cuisine and had a powerful unifying influence on the cooking of this newly-formed nation where the majority of its citizens spoke only their regional dialect and ate only local produce, which remained the case in many parts of Italy until after World War II. By the 13th edition, the recipes increased to 790, based mainly on the food of Tuscany and Artusi's native region, Emilia-Romagna, and included nine using the potato which finally succeeded in making it a respectable food.

Today potatoes are an important part of Italy's agriculture, from Sicily and the South up to the Veneto. This country's relatively gentle climate produces a precocious potato crop, particularly appreciated in northern Europe where much of it is exported. The lagoon area is especially famous for its early potatoes and one of the five principal Italian varieties of this tuber is the QUARANTINA DI CHIOGGIA, reknown for its taste: QUARANTINA indicates that the plant has a brief growing and harvesting cycle— 40 days. In spite of the quality of the local crop, Venetians, like Italians in general, eat fewer potatoes than other Europeans; however, potato dumplings, called GNOCCHI (p. 86) are typically "Veneto". Italians never eat the skin of the potato and are unfamiliar with baked potatoes: the skin is thrown away and friends treat my insistence on its edibleness with patronizing skepticism.

From 1710-1750 animal epidemics killed much of the Veneto's cattle population. To deal with this very serious situation, the Venetian Republic founded a Dept. of Agriculture at the University of Padua, the first of its kind in Europe, & within a few decades farming methods had improved more in the Veneto than anywhere else in Italy. Both theoretical & practical teaching took place & to this day, the Facoltà di Agraria maintains land for experiments & cultivation, along with its academic courses. In the mid 1800's the Dept. assembled a collection of models of farm machines & implements in the interest of public instruction & education. These beautiful wood & iron scale models represent devices used in Europe & North America in the 18th & 19th centuries & faithfully reproduce all of the original's working parts; from these examples, artisans & mechanics were able to build real, functioning machines in their likeness. Today, the 263 miniature machines & tools remain an important testimony of this Dept.'s significant history & of the history of farming in general.

MACHINE FOR CUTTING POTATOES FOR FODDER

Sally Spector

RISI IN CAVROMAN
~ 4 SERVINGS ~

OLIVE OIL

1 medium ONION
1 stalk CELERY } finely chopped
1 large CARROT

1/2 - 3/4 LB. CASTRATED LAMB,* cut into small pieces

1 stick CINNAMON
2 CLOVES

SALT & PEPPER

1/2 cup WHITE WINE

10 OZ. RISO FINO or SUPER-FINO

1 1/2 QT. hot BROTH or WATER ►

2-3 TB. BUTTER

* The meat used for CAVROMAN is cut from the brisket, or breast, PETTO in Italian

► if using BOUILLON, keep the CUBE & WATER separate

For this dish, the MEAT is stewed with the VEGETABLES & SPICES, the RICE is partially cooked & they are cooked together for the final 10-15 minutes of preparation

RICE with CASTRATED LAMB (or BABY GOAT)

1) Cook the ONION, CELERY & CARROT in a small amount of OIL until soft but not browned.

2) Add the MEAT & the dry BOUILLON CUBE & cook, stirring, until lightly browned, & the CUBE dissolves. Mix in the CINNAMON, CLOVES & a dash of SALT & PEPPER.

3) Add the WINE & about 1 cup of BROTH or WATER. Simmer for 1 1/2 - 2 hours, half-covered. It should never get "dry"; if necessary, add a bit more BROTH or WATER.

~ If prepared ahead of time, reheat before continuing ~

4) In another pot, heat about 1 TB. each of OIL & BUTTER & quickly sauté the RICE in it.

5) Add a ladel of hot BROTH or WATER to the RICE & stir constantly, maintaining a medium boil. When the liquid is reduced, add another ladelful, stirring to keep the RICE from sticking to the pot. Continue this process for about 12 minutes, at which point the RICE will be about three-quarters cooked.

6) Add the warm MEAT mixture. Continue adding the BROTH, one ladel at a time, stirring constantly. After 7 or 8 minutes, the RICE should be done. If not, continue cooking, adding a bit of hot WATER if the original quantity is used up.

7) Stir in a TB. or two of BUTTER & serve immediately.

SIOR ANTONIO RIOBA one of the four stone statues known as "I MORI" - the Moors. - representations of Levantine merchants that adorn a building in Campo dei Mori, Cannaregio. They are said to be brothers, who came to Venice from the Peloponneso in 1112, became citizens & were successful merchants. Rioba wears a tight fitting cap; a band around his forehead is attached to a chest resting on his shoulders which would contain the exotic goods from the East he traded in Venice. His left hand holds a small case that probably was used for money, jewels or similar precious things. In 1620 the last member of this family died & his name was given to Rioba who was thus renamed "Antonio" Rioba. Proof of Venetians' affection for I MORI is seen in the fact Rioba was chosen to be their PASQUINO. Pasquino was the name given to the remains of a statue from the 3rd century B.C. discovered during archaeological excavations in Rome in 1501 - Pasquino being the name of a tailor whose shop was near there & who is said to have used the statue for modeling his creations. Renaissance Romans revived an ancient tradition, which continued through the 19th century, of posting anonymous satirical comments - called PASQUINATE - on the statue: defamatory writings about the government, church, private citizens etc. Venetians adopted this practice in the 17th & 18th centuries & hung similar messages on Sior Antonio Rioba who, like Pasquino in Rome, was the "spokesman" for popular, anonymous political satire. This custom has disappeared & Rioba's past social importance is for the most part forgotten.

RISI IN CAVROMAN —rice with stewed castrated lamb— is an old, classic Venetian dish but it is rarely made today. Its ingredients reflect the city's past as a great sea power and the close ties it once had with the Eastern Mediterranean and the spice trade. The origin of the word CAVROMAN is uncertain: it may come from CAPRONE, Italian for male goat (lamb is AGNELLO) and it has been suggested that goat was once used instead of lamb, or perhaps Venetians mistakenly thought that the lamb imported from the East was goat. But, no one really knows for sure, and Boerio's Dictionary of Venetian dialect says CAVROMAN contains castrated lamb or baby goat.

Venice's marine environment meant that meat was never very plentiful here and to this day, Venetians are not big meat eaters. However, two of this city's traditional recipes use castrated lamb, a a meat that was, and still is, common in the Eastern Mediterranean. Venice got it from Dalmatia, the area along the eastern coast of the Adriatic Sea that stretches from the city of Zara down to Montenegro, famous, among other things, for its plentiful flocks of castrated lambs; about 50% of the land there is mountainous, interspersed with high pastures for grazing. Morlacchian nomadic shepherds settled in that region in the 6th century and were joined by Rumanian sheep herders 600 years later and their descendants maintained this way of life for centuries: statistics in the early 1900's showed 2,000 sheep for every 1,000 persons.

By the early 1200's Venice had already attained a position of strength in the Adriatic Sea and this power continued to grow, spreading into the Eastern Mediterranean. Like many other places in that part of the world, Dalmatia became "Venetian-ized": Venetian nobles governed many cities there and the Republic had easy access to a supply of castrated lamb. Venice's activity in the spice trade made it possible to have the other essential ingredients for CAVROMAN— cinnamon and cloves. These two spices, native to South East Asia, were among the most important ones that Venetian traders imported from the East and then, at great profit, exported throughout Europe. (p.163)

SallySpector

Castration takes place when the animal is six weeks old, rendering it more docile. Its physical energy declines, thus it fattens up better, and its meat does not take on the strong taste and odor associated with lamb but instead, becomes extraordinarily delicate and in fact, castrated lamb is highly prized among meats. One of the first books ever printed on how to lead a long, healthy life, Trattato della vita sobria (Treatise on Sober Living), written by the Venetian patrician Alvise Cornaro (1475-1566), recommends this meat, especially for the elderly. In spite of his advice, however, Italians do not eat much of it and its consumption in this country has been mostly limited to Venice and parts of the Veneto. Venetians were eating CASTRÀ—Venetian for CASTRATO or castrated—well before they were eating rice; their combining the two produced RISI IN CAVROMAN and the use of Eastern spices gives this dish an exotic, "Byzantine" character that has virtually disappeared from Venice's cuisine. Today some recipes include tomatoes but this plant from the New World did not become common here until the 1800's, well after the creation of RISI IN CAVROMAN.

The other use of castrated lamb is associated with one of Venice's most solemn holidays, "LA SALUTE", celebrated November 21st commemorating the ending of the last terrible plague that devastated the city from 1630-31. The CASTRÀ is salted, smoked and dried. Modern refrigeration has liberated much of the world from the problems of food spoiling but until the introduction of cold as a means of preservation, the dangers of rotten food were a constant menace: the only methods available for conserving food and preventing it from decaying were drying, salting or smoking. The epidemics and plagues that repeatedly ravaged Europe throughout the Middle Ages and the Renaissance were greatly exacerbated by unsanitary living conditions and the consumption of food gone bad and the Venetian government was always extremely attentive to the perils of importing contaminated fresh meat. A safe alternative was the salted, smoked and sun-dried castrated lamb from Dalmatia and thus it was most appropriate that the traditional dish eaten on "LA FESTA DELLA SALUTE", called CASTRADINA, contains this meat (p.113).

RISOTTO DI PESCE   RICE WITH SEAFOOD

There are numerous recipes for RISOTTO DI PESCE, also called RISOTTO ALLA PESCATORA. It may be made with different types of fish and shellfish, as well as cuttlefish or squid, or it may contain only one of these various forms of seafood. This recipe calls for fish, mollusks and crustaceans —all fresh— and a fundamental ingredient is the homemade broth.

~ 4 SERVINGS ~

1½ LB. each: MUSSELS + CLAMS

¼ LB. BABY SHRIMP, shelled } cut into
 "   "   SOLE   } small
 "   "   BASS or ANGLER   } pieces

4 TB plus a few drops of OLIVE OIL

2 cloves GARLIC, left whole

½ cup dry WHITE WINE

11 OZ. RISO FINO or SUPER FINO

SALT + PEPPER

2-3 TB. minced fresh PARSLEY

✳ 1 QT. FISH BROTH, simmering

✳ 1) Prepare the BROTH: Put the following ingredients in a pot + boil slowly 'til the WATER is reduced by half, about 30 minutes. Strain, pressing the FISH + VEGETABLES to extract all their juices + discard them.

3-4 big FISH HEADS	1 CARROT		1 BAY LAUREL LEAF
8 whole PEPPER GRAINS	1 ONION	left whole	¼ cup dry WHITE WINE
3 sprigs PARSLEY	1 stalk CELERY		2 QT. WATER

2) Clean the MUSSELS + CLAMS: scrub their shells + remove the MUSSELS' "beard". Cook them in a pan with a few drops of OIL, a bit of WATER + a GARLIC clove over medium heat. After 3-4 minutes, they will open. Remove them from the shell + set them aside. Strain their cooking juice + set aside. Discard the shells.

3) Heat the OIL in a large pot + gently cook the second clove of GARLIC. When it starts to color, discard it.

4) Add the pieces of FISH, the SHRIMP + the WINE. When the WINE has evaporated, add the strained CLAM + MUSSEL juice.

5) Add the RICE + mix it in well with the other ingredients. Stirring constantly, add a ladel of BROTH + when the mixture becomes "dry", add another ladel of BROTH. Continue for about 15 minutes + then add the CLAMS + MUSSELS. Cook for another 3-4 minutes, adding BROTH, stirring constantly, 'til the RICE is "AL DENTE".

6) Taste for SALT + PEPPER. Sprinkle with PARSLEY + serve immediately.

CAMPO DEI FRARI
SAN POLO

Grain & Pasta — Grano e Pasta

About 10,000 years ago, in Mesopotamia, people discovered that planting was a more reliable source of food than hunting and their transition from a nomadic to an agricultural society is considered one of the most significant developments in human history. Since then, cereals, especially rice, millet, barley and corn, have been mankind's major source of nourishment and important foods for animals as well. They also had great social and political importance since, for centuries, the security of cities depended greatly on a sufficient supply of grain: some form of bread was the staple of most people's diet.

From the beginning, Venice's leaders realized that a state is strong and healthy only if its citizens are protected and have enough to eat. They knew that lack of food could lead to social unrest and spoiled food made people more vulnerable to the devastating plagues that were a constant threat during the Middle Ages and the Renaissance. Throughout its long life, one of the Venetian Republic's chief priorities was to keep the city stocked with grains — mostly wheat and millet. The Venetians did not sow and harvest grain but instead had to exchange goods for it, or buy it with money, which singled them out as a very strange race in the eyes of

others. They imported some of it from the cities of Ferrara, Mantova, Pavia and Piacenza but much of it came from outside Italy. Transport by water was easier and cheaper than by land and by the 1200's, Venetian round-bottomed ships were sailing much of the Mediterranean — to Sicily, Albania, Crete and Egypt — to procure wheat which they brought to the GRANAI PUBBLICI, or the Public Granaries, the most important of which were at San Marco and the Rialto.

Private citizens could buy this grain and some of it was allotted to the city's pastry makers but at least half of it was reserved for Venice's bakers of bread, who belonged to one of the city's oldest organized professions, divided into two groups. The FORNERI baked the dough that they themselves prepared, as well as

WHEAT from south façade of the Church of Santa Maria dei Miracoli built 1481-89 by Pietro Lombardo (1435-1515), in Castello

dough mixed by others brought to them to be baked; they could not sell directly to the public and were known as PANICUOCOLI, meaning those who "bake bread dough prepared by other people". The PISTORI, instead, baked and sold both their bread and that of the FORNERI.

PUTTO HOLDING WHEAT from painting by Paolo Veronese (1528-1588), "Hercules & Ceres Pay Homage to Venice". This allegory, done for the ceiling of the room where the Magistrates of the Granai Pubblici met, is now in the Gallerie dell' Accademia.

Sally Spector

The FORNERI and the PISTORI were subject to a variety of punishments if they did not adhere to certain State imposed ordinances. If they made bread from wheat that had not been controlled or with sub-standard flour, it was confiscated, cut into pieces and thrown on the steps of the Rialto Bridge; thus, they were publicly disgraced. If bread lacked the government seal or was of unsatisfactory quality —poorly baked or with uneven, irregular consistency— it was sequestered. If it was below required weight, the guilty baker had to pay a fine for each delinquent loaf; documents show that selling underweight

bread was one of the most common crimes committed during the Middle Ages all over Europe and the Venetian government was constantly on guard for such fraudulent products.

The grain in the GRANAI PUBBLICI not only served Venice's alimentary needs; it was also an important commodity of exchange, whose value often increased substantially, and its condition was carefully monitored. Every day, a special committee of the Grain Office informed the Doge on how much of it there was and it was periodically aired to prevent

CA
DEL

CAMPIELLO DEL PISTOR near Campo
San Polo, where Rio de San Polo, Rio de San
Stin + Rio de Sant'Augustin all meet.
The word PISTOR, once synonymous in Venice
for a baker of bread, comes from the Latin word
PISTORI, meaning those who ground grain in
a mortar. The word remains part of this city's
toponomy but its significance has been forgotten.

dampness and mold and to get rid of insects. It was a necessity, not a luxury; when periods of drought or extreme winter temperatures caused crops to fail, the Venetian State reaped huge profits from selling its grain reserves which could be stockpiled for relatively long periods of time: millet, considered mankind's most ancient food, can be preserved for more than 100 years. As an example of this commerce, 60,000 tons of wheat were shipped to Venice over a 12 month period in the early 1500's, deemed more than enough to feed 300,000 for one year. The city's population was then 150,000 so there was gain to be made and plenty of grain left for Venetians; the Rialto, in fact, was one of Europe's chief grain markets.

Bread is not the only important use for wheat in Italy; the other, of course, is PASTA. Venice, as already mentioned, is famous for its rice dishes and does not have a characteristic PASTA. The most common types eaten here are a short form, called SUBIOTO, used in the bean soup PASTA E FASIOI; long, thick whole wheat SPAGHETTI, called BIGOLI, served with an onion and anchovy sauce; and the classic Neapolitan SPAGHETTI — the recipes for these dishes follow. Flour figures in another guise in Venetian first courses in the form of GNOCCHI, or dumplings, made from flour, potatoes, and sometimes, the pulp of fresh pumpkin (p. 86, 89)

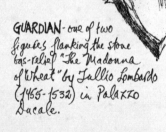

GUARDIAN - one of two figures flanking the stone bas-relief "The Madonna of Wheat" by Jullio Lombardo (1455-1532) in Palazzo Ducale.

The lack of a characteristic local bread here, as is found in most places in Italy, is often said to be due to the fact that for centuries, Venetians have been eating POLENTA as a substitute. A few of the most common breads — mostly rolls - are illustrated; they are distinguished more by their shapes and names than by their taste.

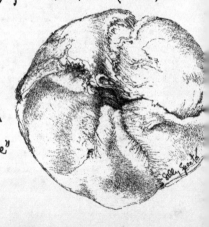

LA ROSETTA

"little rose"

Fig. 3   *a*

WATER MILL ON A BOAT

The MILLER stands in one of the doorways. The "HOUSE" contains sacks of grain & his bed.

a) MILL ON A BOAT
d) COLUMN for winding rope
e) PEGS for attaching rope
f) DOOR
g) DECK with Miller
h) SAILS

Mills have been operating since at least the 1st century B.C. but were not common until the Middle Ages. At first they were used almost exclusively for grinding grain but eventually became the principal "motorized" energy of pre-industrial society & by the 12th century windmills were almost as numerous as watermills. The hundreds of mills in the Veneto (there were 4,000 in 1766) included a third type: FLOATING MILLS, or MULINI NATANTI, made entirely of wood, consisting of one or more boats, completely covered with black tar to be impermeable. Movable, they could be positioned in any direction in order to exploit water currents but were usually fixed with anchors or tied to river banks with ropes or chains. Since they obstructed & interfered with boat traffic, most of them were eliminated after World War I; the last ones were on the River Adige, southwest of Chioggia.

from Dizionario delle arti e de' mestieri *by Francesco Griselini & Marco Fassadoni; 18 vols. Printed in 1771, in Venice, by Modesto Fenzo (Marciana Library)*

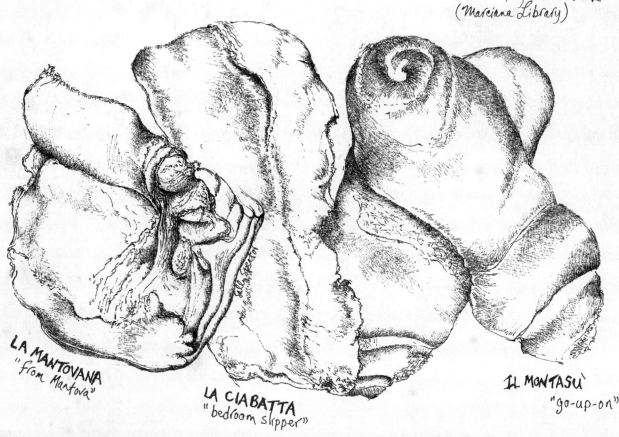

LA MANTOVANA
"from Mantova"

LA CIABATTA
"bedroom slipper"

IL MONTASÙ
"go-up-on"

Marco Polo (1256-1324), the great Venetian merchant and traveler, is usually given credit for having introduced PASTA to Italy, for it is often assumed he brought it to Venice when he returned from the Far East in 1295. However, scholars point out that this food is not mentioned in the famous narration of his voyage, Il Milion; since he paid close attention to the unfamiliar things that he saw natives eating during the years he spent crossing Asia, from 1271 to 1295, he undoubtedly would have included some reference to it. He did write, though, that in Sumatra he saw people eating something resembling what "we make with wheat flour", interpreted as being similar to the very wide, flat form of LASAGNE.

Proof that historians use to show that there definitely was PASTA in Italy prior to Polo's return lies in a document from 1279, an inventory that a notary in Genoa made of a client's worldly goods which includes a case of MACCHERONI. But, much older evidence decorates

BAS-RELIEF from Venetian Byzantine arch, 12-13th cent. in Corte Seconda del Milion, site of Marco Polo's house near Teatro Malibran, Cannaregio

one of the most important tombs in the Etruscan necropolis of Cervéteri, north of Rome near the Tyrrhenian Sea. This site has frescoes and stucco work that depict domestic objects, including the utensils employed in making PASTA: a rolling pin for rolling out the dough, the board to do this on and the knives for cutting it. Thus, PASTA has been eaten in Italy since at least the 6th century B.C., although its dominant role in this nation's cuisine began more recently than is usually imagined.

Perhaps more intriguing than PASTA's history is why, considering that wheat is grown all over the world except in humid, tropical zones and, along with rice, is one of the worlds most important alimentary plants, did PASTA become so much more important in Italy than in other places? The answer may lie in this country's singular climate and geology which are ideally suited for producing this food.

Among the thousands of varieties of cereal grasses included in the wheat family, there are two principal types. One is soft wheat, or GRANO TENERO (*Triticum vulgare*) which has from eight to ten percent of the elastic protein called gluten and is used mainly for making bread, cookies and cakes while the other, hard wheat, or GRANO DURO (*Triticum durum*), has from eleven to fifteen percent gluten.

The strong gluten in hard wheat comes from semolina, which is the purified middlings that are produced when it is milled. These granular particles contain nutritive plant tissue, called endosperm, which is necessary for making PASTA but unsatisfactory for making bread; vice versa, soft wheat is not suitable for making PASTA. Hard wheat does not disintegrate when it is boiled, as does soft wheat, and when cooked correctly, does not become mushy. Another difference between them is where they grow. Soft wheat thrives in cold, wet climates that hard wheat cannot tollerate;

GRANO DURO needs the warm, dry conditions of Italy, Greece and North Africa.

Thus, Italy has the single essential ingredient, but having the grain is not enough: water is also fundamental and Italy's is considered to be perfect for making PASTA. In fact, some of the world's most renowned PASTA factories are in the Abruzzo region, which lies along the Adriatic Sea in the south eastern part of central Italy; a group of rugged mountains there, called La Maiella, which are part of the Apennines, reaches heights of almost 3,000 meters and this particular geological formation, with its underground springs and abundant snow, is responsible for producing this highly prized water, which, combined with hard wheat flour, creates a unique PASTA dough.

The drying process is also crucial; once formed into its particular shape, the dough must dry without fermenting or getting moldy and this greatly depends on the balance between the temperature of the air and its humidity content.

The moisture in the dough must be reduced slowly and gradually —if dried too quickly, it cracks, if too slowly, it stretches and gets musty— and it turns out that the gentle sea breezes that parts of southern Italy, especially around Naples, receive, make for exceptionally favorable drying conditions.

In spite of these natural factors, PASTA did not become Italy's national food until relatively recently. For centuries, it was something special, reserved for the wealthy or eaten only on holidays and momentous occasions since very few people could afford the time and manual labor necessary for making it on a regular basis. It was only with the Industrial Revolution that PASTA became "common", when, step by step, machines began to do what previously had been done by hand. In the early 1800's, in Naples, the up and down movement of a piston in a somewhat primitive, mostly wooden screw press extruded shaped PASTA and in 1830, a kneading machine prepared the dough and these methods were then adopted in Liguria and Sicily. Experimentation continued and in 1870, in Naples, an hydraulic press replaced the screw one and then a more modern kneading machine finally made mass production possible.

The drying process also became mechanized —a sort of merry-go-round was even tried— and around 1900 a hot air technique was perfected. Although these technical advancements succeeded in making PASTA more available and its consumption spread, it was still expensive and remained a luxury product, to be bought with money and not exchanged for something. Poorer people only began eating it in the early 1900's and it did not become an everyday food in the Veneto until after the Second World War. Today it is very much a part of Venetian cuisine and many people eat just as much PASTA as they eat rice.... and perhaps, more.

PASTA E FASIOI

This soup can be made from either fresh or dried beans. DO NOT USE CANNED OR FROZEN BEANS because neither their texture nor taste can produce a true PASTA E FASIOI. In Venice, fresh LAMON and BORLOTTI beans, in their brightly colored pods, are available from May through September. They can be stored for up to three weeks in the pod, but once fresh beans are shelled, they should be refrigerated and eaten within 48 hours. Dried beans, sold loose, not packaged, are almost always available. They should be eaten within a year from when picked and stored in a cool dry place, exposed to the air. Not surprisingly, fresh beans make a more liquidy soup than dried ones, which have lost much of their moisture. For a soup that a spoon can stand up in, dried beans must be used. Some people always prefer dried beans as they believe they have more flavor than the younger, fresh ones.

PASTA & BEAN SOUP

The PASTA used for this soup should be a short form: the most traditional one is called SUBIOTO, which is like a short RIGATONE. SPAGHETTI are not recommended, because even if they are broken into small strips, they are too "thin". Long, wide PASTA, like TAGLIATELLE or PAPPARDELLE (from PAPPARE, meaning to eat in a gorging, devouring manner) should be broken before cooking: it can be frustrating, and difficult, to scoop up long, slithery noodles with a spoon. The important thing is to choose a shape that has a firm consistency so it can "hold" the thick soup and can also easily be eaten with a spoon.

PASTA E FASIOI is eaten hot, tepid, at room temperature....depending on personal preference and/or circumstances. North Americans, and northern Europeans, tend to like their soup hotter than Italians do.

THE RECIPE FOR THIS DISH IS ON PAGE 83

Bean   FAGIOLO fasioi   fam Leguminosae, Phaseolus valgaris

The derivation of the word bean is uncertain, although some etymologists believe it comes from the Indo-European BHABHA, meaning bean; it may also be the source for FAVA, the Italian word for broad bean. The Greek PHASELOS and the Latin PHASEOLUS gave birth to FAGIOLO, while the Latin verb LEGERE, meaning to gather, is the root for LEGUME, the family to which beans belong.

It is said that it is thanks to beans that PASTA entered the kitchens of the Veneto: one of this region's most traditional dishes is PASTA E FASIOI, a thick soup made of boiled beans and PASTA; before PASTA became common it was made with barley or rice. Its humble ingredients qualify it as rustic, peasant cuisine —for centuries, legumes were disdained by the wealthy— and in Venice this dish was associated with poor people and the tavern-like establishments called OSTERIE where there was always a big pot of PASTA E FASIOI, sometimes so thick that a spoon could stand up in it, eaten at all hours of the day and night. Haute-cuisine discovered it after World War II and now it is celebrated for its tastiness and authenticity and is enjoyed by all social classes.

Beans are among the world's most common foods —there are more than 150 species— and one of the most valuable as well. Nicknamed the "poor man's meat", they are a rich source of protein; if dried, they can be ground into flour and mixed with grains to make bread or stored for winter months when fresh vegetables are scarce. Scientific research shows

FARMER from a capital of the arcade of Palazzo Ducale. The original (1340-1355) in the Palazzo Museum is headless; the 19th cent. copy outside, instead, has a head.

that their protein is incomplete, being low in an essential amino acid, but that combining them with certain foods such as cereals, like PASTA or rice, completes it so that all their nutritional value becomes accessible. Thus, there is instinctive, rural wisdom in a dish of PASTA E FASIOI which combines two vital classes of foods: carbohydrates and proteins.

Beans grow in many parts of the world and have been cultivated for thousands of years but those that Venetians eat today, and which make their bean soup so delicious, are not the ones that ancient Romans and medieval peasants ate. Many regions of Italy have a characteristic bean soup: the Veneto version is distinguished by the LAMON or BORLOTTO bean, both comparable to the cranberry bean. Lamon and Borlotti beans owe their origins to South America, a King, a Pope and a Renaissance humanist, Piero Valeriano (1477-1558), from Belluno, a small city about 100 kms. north of Venice, under Venetian domain from 1404-1797. During his lifetime, Valeriano was a highly esteemed scholar of Greek and Latin: he wrote an encyclopedia called Hierogliphica, which compares the significance of various symbols with hieroglyphics, as well as prose and poetry in Latin and one such poem, "De milacis cultura", contains the first precise description of the germination and cultivation of the new South American beans. He was also the private tutor of Pope Clement the Seventh's relatives, Ippolito and Alessandro de' Medici and was well-known at the Papal Court in Rome and it was this connection that brought beans into his life.

OLLA a somewhat rough-hewn ceramic container used by ancient & medieval peoples which served for both cooking & conserving food. This example, from the late 1300's, found at Malamocco in the south lagoon, was probably made in Venice. The lid was found on the island of San Francesco del Deserto, near Burano. (Soprintendenza per i Beni Ambientali e Architettonici di Venezia)

Sally Spector

South American beans were among the treasures that explorers brought back with them from the New World to present to the King of Spain, Charles V, and he, in turn, gave a sack of them to the Medici Pope, Clement VII, who offered them to Ippolito and Alessandro's tutor. The Medici family was also responsible for the introduction of these beans into France, for it seems that Catherine de' Medici took some with her as part of her dowry when she married the future King of France, Henry II, in 1553, which indicates the value that these new legumes had then. Valeriano took them to the town of Lamon, about 30 kms. west of Belluno, where he gave them to local farmers to plant; cultivation began in the early 1530's and beans gradually replaced peas, which had previously been the dominant crop there. The foreign plant's superiority was quickly apparent, valued especially for its resistence to parasites and its ability to grow amidst other crops, thus making it possible to raise a variety of produce.

F A G G I V O L I

BEANS, woodcut from Herbario Nuovo by Cesare Durante (1523-1590), born in Rome. Trained as a physician, he was Pope Sixtus the Fifth's private doctor but he was also an amateur botanist as well as a poet & is probably best remembered for his Herbario, first printed in 1585, in Rome; published often in the 1600's, it was last printed in Venice in 1718. Although not very innovative, this book was extremely popular. It includes all known medical plants of Europe & the East & West Indies. In addition to scientific information, the plants' "rare secrets" & their "singular remedies for curing the most troublesome infirmities are described. From the edition printed in Venice, in 1636 by Giunti. (Correr Library)

Sally Spector

In Venice, however, these new American beans were initially appreciated for their aesthetic qualities rather than for their alimentary ones and were called FAGIOLI TURCHI because of their distant provenance. The adjective "Turkish," which in the 1500's was synonymous for the unfamiliar and exotic, was used for many of the new and strange foods introduced into Europe from the New World. Venetians grew these beans in pots on their balconies, as this plant's beautiful leaves and tall stalk made it ornamental as well as a welcome source of shade.

Pope Clement's gift to Valeriano was, along with commissioning Michelangelo to design the new Sacristy of the Church of San Lorenzo in Florence with the Medici tombs, one of the few positive things that occurred during his politically disasterous reign. The Bellunesi farmers succeeded in developing two new beans which they named LAMON, in honor of where they were created and first planted, and BORLOTTO, from the northern Italian dialect word BORLÒT, meaning rounded. Venetians used to call them "SCOZZESE", or "Scottish", perhaps because of the variegated colors of these beans: Italians say "SCOZZESE" to mean "plaid", the barred and striped pattern fabric of various colors associated with Scottish Highlanders.

Although the LAMON is considered more "refined" than the BORLOTTO, both are acclaimed for their taste; they are also quite beautiful. Both the pods and the individual beans, which vary from an off-white to beige in color, are mottled with irregular spots and vein-like markings. The pods are more spectacular, ranging in color from bright pink to magenta and purple. while the beans, though remarkable, seem subdued in comparison; their burgundy speckles disappear when cooked and produce a soup of a warm reddish-brown tone... I wish they could somehow retain their spots, for the soup, full of such decorated beans, would be stunning...

As with other prized Italian food products, geography plays an important part in the life of these beans. The high plateau of Lamon, once the site of a glacial lake, lies at an elevation of 600 meters and is extremely fertile. The mountains that surround it made it difficult to get there until the 20th century, when modern roads were built, but they also protect it and keep its climate very temperate. These soil and weather conditions are responsible in part for one of the most appreciated characteristics of these beans: they have a very thin skin, making them easily digestible.

Today, authentic Lamon and Borlotti beans are grown only within a circumscribed zone on small, family-operated farms. The plants are not chemically treated and their cultivation is strictly controlled in order to maintain the recognized excellence of the beautiful beans that now bring fame and fortune to an area that suffered great poverty and hardship in the past.

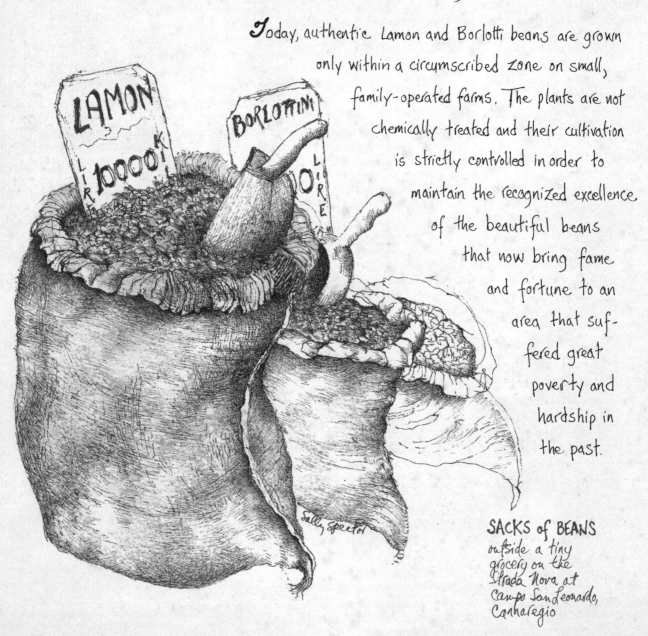

SACKS of BEANS
outside a tiny
grocery on the
Strada Nova at
Campo San Leonardo,
Cannaregio

PASTA E FASIOI   PASTA AND BEAN SOUP

~ 4 SERVINGS ~

2 LB. fresh } BEANS { LAMON,
OR   BORLOTTI,
1 LB. dried }   CRANBERRY

Shell the BEANS. If dried BEANS are used, soak them in 1½ quarts tepid WATER for 12 hours to soften them. Soaking also prevents their skins from bursting while they cook.

4-5 cups cold WATER — Some people use the BEANS' soaking WATER, others prefer fresh WATER.

1 medium ONION } left whole,
1 medium CARROT }   not
1 stalk CELERY } sliced

sprig of fresh ROSEMARY

5 OZ. short form PASTA — not EGG PASTA !

SALT   PEPPER   OLIVE OIL

{ ~ OPTIONAL INGREDIENTS ~
a second ONION, stuck with a few CLOVES
a small piece of PANCETTA, LARD or BACON }

1) Put the WATER in a big, heavy pot & add the ONION(S), CARROT, CELERY, BEANS, ROSEMARY & PORK. Bring to a rapid boil. Cover & cook at a slow boil for about 2 hours 'til the BEANS are quite soft.

2) Discard the cloved ONION. Grind the VEGETABLES & about ⅓ of the BEANS in a food mill, then put them back into the pot with the rest of the BEANS. The soup should be thick: consistency depends on the quantity of BEANS pureed. DO NOT GRIND TOO MANY — the texture of PASTA E FASIOI is a combination of the dense liquid, the whole BEANS & the PASTA.

3) Bring the soup to boiling & add the PASTA. Cook 'til the PASTA is done, about 10-15 minutes. Turn off heat & let sit for 15 minutes, covered, before serving. Season with SALT & PEPPER.

Many people pour a few drops of OLIVE OIL into their PASTA E FASIOI before eating it.

BIGOLI IN SALSA   WHOLEWHEAT SPAGHETTI WITH ANCHOVIES & ONIONS

Venetian cooking has produced fewer pasta dishes than anywhere else in Italy but BIGOLI IN SALSA is so good that it virtually makes up for this lack. It is very simple in both preparation and ingredients, which include long, dark wholewheat spaghetti called BIGOLI. BIGOLI are typically "VENETI"; outside of Venice, in places like Verona, Vicenza and Bassano del Grappa, they are eaten with meat and game sauces but in Venice the SALSA is always made with anchovies and onions. BIGOLI are sometimes called MORI, from the Greek word MAUROS and the Latin MAURU, meaning dark; the inhabitants of Mauretania – the ancient country and Roman province in north west Africa, today Algeria and Morocco — a Moslem people of Arab and Berber origins who invaded

Sally Spector

Spain in 711, were known as MORI, or Moors. Shakespeare's Othello is probably the most famous Moor associated with Venice; others are the two bronze figures who strike the bell on the Clock Tower in Piazza San Marco and the stone sculptures in the Campo dei Mori in Cannaregio (p.62). The word MORO is also the common adjective for a dark complexion or dark hair.

BIGOLI IN SALSA is eaten throughout the year but it was once a common dish for the days on which the Church prohibited meat, such as Ash Wednesday and Good Friday; it is still traditional to eat it on Christmas Eve.

PALAZZO CONTARINI-FASAN, c.1450, on the Grand Canal facing the Salute Church. Legend says this was the home of Desdemona, Othello's wife. The Contarini were one of Venice's oldest greatest families: FASAN, Venetian for FAGIANO, or pheasant may refer to a Contarini's love

~ 4 SERVINGS ~

½ cup OLIVE OIL

2 large ONIONS - halved & sliced very thin. Some people use 4 or 5 ONIONS...

5-6 ANCHOVY fillets - from tin or jar

1) Heat the OIL very hot in a large skillet.

2) Add the ONIONS & immediately lower the heat. Cook them, uncovered, very slowly, until withered & transparent. THEY MUST NOT BURN: to avoid this, add a spoonful or two of water if necessary. Stir occasionally.

3) When the ONIONS are wilted, stir in the ANCHOVIES. Cook very slowly until the ANCHOVIES can be easily mashed with a wooden spoon. They should "dissolve" into the ONIONS 'til the mixture takes on a smooth paste-like consistency & becomes light brown in color. When done, add a dash of PEPPER, turn off heat & cover.

✳ The sauce may be prepared while the WATER boils for the BIGOLI or it may be prepared ahead of time. It should be gently reheated before combining with the pasta.

1 LB. wholewheat SPAGHETTI ("BIGOLI")

2-3 Tb. minced fresh PARSLEY

freshly ground PEPPER

4) Bring a large quantity of lightly salted WATER to a rapid boil (ANCHOVIES are salty), then put in the SPAGHETTI. They will begin to soften almost immediately & by gently stirring them they will completely submerge into the water. Stir occasionally to keep them from sticking together. Boil 'til done: cooking time depends on personal taste. Italians prefer their pasta, like their rice, AL DENTE, with a slight bite to it, never soft or mushy.

5) Drain the SPAGHETTI & stir them immediately into the warm ANCHOVY & ONION sauce. Sprinkle with PARSLEY and serve.

The traditional long, thick, dark BIGOLO was hollow inside. Today it is very difficult to find, & now BIGOLI are more like SPAGHETTI. Wholewheat pasta is usually cooked a bit longer than white pasta.

BIGOLARO instrument for making BIGOLI. Operated like a press, the BIGOLI were extruded through the holes in the disc. From a 19th c. example in the Museum of Agricultural Life in Susegana, near Conegliano

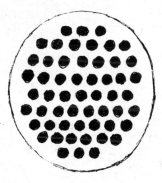

Dumplings ~   Gnochi ~

GNOCHI are small, oval dumplings. The word comes from the Lombards, the ancient Germanic tribe that invaded northern Italy in the 5th century and settled there. Their word KNOHHA, meaning knot or knuckle, gave birth to the low German word KNÖKLE which became GNOCCO in Italian, GNOCO in Venetian. GNOCHI made from a mixture of flour and water, or sometimes milk, were eaten in the Veneto as early as the 1500's but they were greatly improved in the 1700's when much of the flour was replaced by mashed potatoes. In some parts of Italy GNOCCHI are made with semolina, but the potato version, extolled for its distinctive taste and consistency, is considered one of the triumphs of the CUCINA VENETA.

GNOCHI DE PATATE   POTATO DUMPLINGS

~ 4 SERVINGS ~

3 LB. old, floury POTATOES, washed but not peeled

3 cups FLOUR

2 EGGS

a pinch of SALT

DISH TOWEL, sprinkled with FLOUR

large pot of lightly SALTED BOILING WATER

6-8 TB. BUTTER
a few fresh SAGE leaves } heated together

(OPTIONAL: freshly grated PARMESAN CHEESE)

1) Boil the POTATOES 'til soft. Drain + peel them: the skin slips off easily under cool running water.

2) Mash the POTATOES + using one's hands, mix them together with the FLOUR, EGGS + SALT until they form a smooth, homogeneous dough.

3) With the hands, sprinkled with FLOUR, make long rolls about 3/4 inch thick + cut them into GNOCHI about one inch long. Press each GNOCO with the curved prongs of a fork + then place them on the spread-out towel. They should not touch each other.

4) Put the GNOCHI in the boiling WATER, + continue boiling 'til they rise to the surface — after about 4 minutes of cooking. Remove with a slotted spoon + serve hot with a spoonful or two of the BUTTER-SAGE mixture + if desired, grated PARMESAN CHEESE.

Fresh GNOCHI are available in Venice's "fresh pasta" stores + some bread shops offer them once a week, usually on Thursday or Friday. They should be refrigerated + eaten within a day or two. They are delicious with just melted butter but tomato + meat sauces also go very well with them.

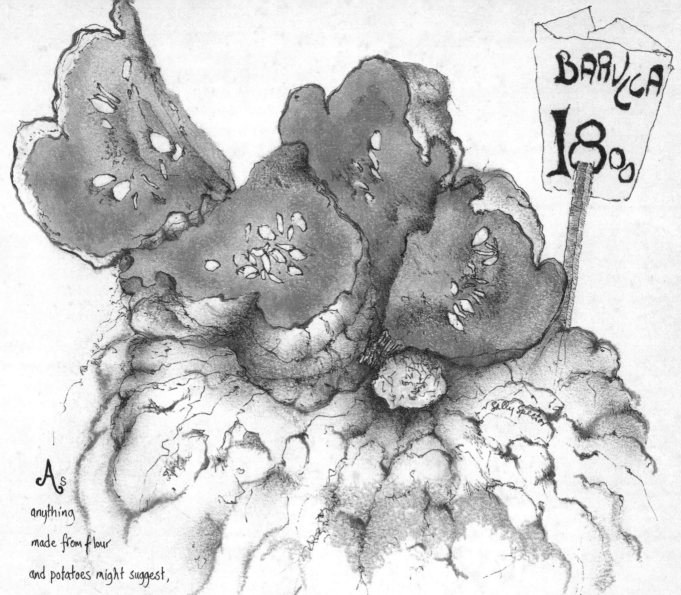

BARUCA
18 00

$\mathcal{A}$s
anything
made from flour
and potatoes might suggest,
GNOCHI DE PATATE can be quite filling and if not prepared correctly – if, for example, too much flour is used – they are
heavy and tough. If made correctly, they are amazingly light and delicate. This recipe depends not on exact measurements
but on relative proportions: intuitive judgment is more important than mathematical precision. The world's most
beautiful GNOCHI are no doubt eaten during the fall and winter when the pumpkins grown in the lagoon are
picked; this gourd's brilliant orange pulp is cooked and mashed with potato, creating an extraordinary color.

$\mathcal{E}$tymologists believe the Italian word for pumpkin – ZUCCA – derives from CUCUTIA, Latin for gourds, or from TUCCA,
Latin for head; in fact, Italians jokingly say ZUCCA for head, or TESTA, and ZUCCHETTA is a skullcap. "Pumpkin"
comes from the old French POMPON, the ornamental tuft on hats, slippers and uniforms, and derives from the Greek
PEPON and the Latin PEPO, meaning "cooked by the sun". The French call pumpkins COURGES and the Venetians
say SUCA. There is no Italian term for the American Indian word "squash": all gourds are ZUCCHE in Italy,
as seen by the fact that ZUCCHINE, or zucchini, which are a squash, are named "little pumpkins". In general,

Although ZUCCHE were grown in the lagoon before the 1500's, the ones cultivated today are native to Central and South America. Italians consider only those gourds with a farinaceous, not stringy pulp to be good eating. One of these is the SUCA SANTA (Cucurbita moschata), also called MARINA DI CHIOGGIA. It is elongated, rounded and flask-like; its smooth skin is yellow-beige with a faint greenish tinge. Older friends of mine remember using the SANTA when learning to swim in the lagoon: two dried SANTE were tied together and hung around the neck to keep one afloat. But, they are far more valued for their taste than as life preservers and some Venetians believe that the SANTA is the best pumpkin for making GNOCHI. The lagoon's other main ZUCCA is the SUCA BARUCA (Cucurbita maxima): dark green with a very hard, knobby rind, shaped like a slightly flattened sphere. Its bumpy skin gave rise to its musical name: BARUCA derives from the Latin word VERRUCA, meaning protuberance. Grown throughout Italy, it is called by dozens of different names, but its gnarled appearance is unmistakable. Since it has a high sugar content, it used to be eaten as a sweet here. Some people recall hearing Venetian street vendors cry "SUCA BARUCA, SUCA BARUCA"; they walked around the city carrying a simple wooden plank and a trestle on which they sliced pieces of baked or roasted pumpkin, ready to eat.

There were tiny stands at the foot of the Rialto Bridge, in addition to the peddlers, where women, and sometimes girls, sold this treat every evening to workers on their way home; this tradition disappeared in the mid-1900's replaced by a seemingly endless choice of "modern" sweets.

American pumpkins can be used to make GNOCHI, but since they tend to have a high water content, more flour may be necessary in order to achieve the right consistency; they thus become rather heavy. This characteristic may be due to the fact that Americans prize big pumpkins. Size is less of a factor for Italians who often exploit gourds' vine-growing ability and cultivate them on trellises, producing smaller, lighter pumpkins.

GNOCHI DE SUCA
POTATO & PUMPKIN DUMPLINGS
~4 SERVINGS~

2 LB. fresh PUMPKIN (c. 2½ cups mashed)

3 large old POTATOES

SALT   ⟨OPTIONAL: 1 EGG⟩

✳ FLOUR - as necessary

6-8 TB. melted BUTTER

c. 6 TB. freshly grated PARMESAN cheese

large pot of briskly boiling salted WATER for step 6.

Venetians use only one type of POTATO for GNOCHI, known as PATATA OLANDESE, or Dutch potato. It is light brown, large, & rather long, an old POTATO with a very floury consistency. Even when raw, one can see that its flesh is dry & powdery. In the markets it is often marked "GNOCHI."

✳ ⟨ FOR LIGHT, TENDER, DELICATE GNOCHI
    USE AS LITTLE FLOUR AS POSSIBLE ⟩

1) Remove the PUMPKIN'S seeds, cut its pulp into small pieces & steam or bake until soft. DO NOT BOIL IT! This makes it absorb water, thus more FLOUR would be necessary to counteract this moisture & the GNOCHI would become tough & heavy.

2) Boil the POTATOES whole, with the skin on: the skin preserves flavor (& vitamins). When soft, rinse them in cold water — the skin slips off easily.

3) In a large bowl or on a flat surface, mash the PUMPKIN & POTATOES together with a pinch of SALT to a smooth, uniform consistency. Some people add a beaten EGG as a binder but others feel its odor is too strong for the PUMPKIN'S delicate flavor.

4) Sprinkle FLOUR, a bit at a time, over & into the mixture, working it in by hand. The amount of FLOUR necessary is determined by how moist the PUMPKIN-POTATO mixture is: it should be just dry enough to knead without sticking to one's fingers & so that it can be formed into a long, roll-like shape, about ¾ of an inch in diameter. Its surface will not be smooth, but rather jagged & uneven.

5) Using a fork — the prongs horizontal, not vertical — cut the roll into pieces about ½ inch wide. The slightly curved prongs cut more gently than a knife. The GNOCHI will be irregularly shaped.

6) One by one, put the GNOCHI in the boiling WATER; they will immediately sink to the bottom. Since they need room to "swim" & they swell a bit in cooking, the pot should never contain more than one layer of them at a time. After a few minutes, they will rise to the surface, the sign that they are done & ready to be removed with a slotted spoon.

7) Serve immediately with melted BUTTER & PARMESAN cheese.

GNOCHI MUST BE EATEN WARM. I have heard how, when eating GNOCHI at home, one person was served at a time while the others waited patiently for their portion. To avoid this situation, in order for everyone to eat together, the GNOCHI can be put in a heated oven as soon as they are done to be kept warm until they are all prepared. Or, they can be made ahead of time, placed on a cookie sheet — without touching each other — & reheated in the oven just before serving.

FONDAMENTA & RIO DEL MEGIO
or millet... in Italian, MIGLIO.
The building behind the
tree, on the right, used to
be the Republic's Millet
Granary, the DEPOSITI DEL
MEGIO, dating back at
least to the 1400's. This
grain was an important
food for Venetians, used
mostly for making bread.
The DEPOSITI, which face
on to the Grand Canal,
now house a public
elementary school: near
San Giacomo da l'Orio,
in Santa Croce.

Polenta

EL TOCIO is a word one often hears Venetians use with regard to food and even before it is clear what it means, it is obviously something extremely good. It is the juice, or INTINGOLO, that the stewing of meat, fowl and fish produces and it is sometimes more delicious and desirable than the main ingredient. Venetians have made an art out of eating EL TOCIO: they soak it up with POLENTA. In fact, it is difficult to imagine food in Venice without it.

In Latin POLENTA means toasted barley flour and the word probably derives from PULVIS and POLLIS, meaning dust and pollin. Today POLENTA is virtually synonymous for cornmeal in both Italian and English but for centuries it referred to a sort of porridge made of water and coarsely ground grain, usually barley, spelt, millet or emmer, also known as FARRO. The combination of these cereals with water was a fundamental source of nourishment for ancient peoples and the history of such concoctions provides insight into what Italians have eaten for the past 2,000 years. Why the word POLENTA is now limited to just cornmeal is due to various factors that were greatly influenced by the Venetian Republic and will be briefly explained.

Within the hierarchy of grains, wheat is supreme: it is the most nutricious, it threshes free from its chaff and because it grinds to a very fine consistency and combines with yeast, it can be used for a variety of foods, from bread to PASTA to sweets. Once it grew throughout much of Italy, but its use was rather limited: the ancient Romans ate bread made from wheat, instead of barley, only for special occasions and Roman soldiers ate POLENTA made

partly with wheat. As that Empire declined, so did wheat production, and with the barbarian invasions in the 5th century, this plant virtually disappeared as its cultivation was progressively abandoned. Only in southern Italy and Sicily, where political and social conditions were very different, did it continue to be harvested.

The Goths, Lombards and other northern tribes who settled in Italy planted inferior, less nutricious grains that are easier to grow and require less care, such as rye, millet, sorghum, spelt and fox-tail millet, some of which are described as being, if not actually harmful, exceedingly bad tasting. Sometimes beans, chick peas and other legumes were added but they did not necessarily make things more appetizing. Flavor, however, was secondary. The essential thing was to have some-thing to eat, to defend one-self against hunger and famine; goodness and quality were less important than quantity, security and ease of produc-tion. But these crops, too, suffered an invasion, this time meteorological. In the late Middle

Ages Europe's weather turned damper and colder and from about 1300 to 1500 temperatures dropped, making farmland less fertile and yields smaller. In addition, seemingly uninterrupted wars meant that planting was neglected, causing workable land to degenerate into swamps; such conflicts, along with repeated plagues and epidemics, significantly reduced the manual labor needed for farming and food for ordinary people was in terribly short supply.

When thinking about Venetian food and its past one tends to ignore historic reality and instead, to imagine the grand banquets seen in Renaissance paintings... I had never thought about what Venetians really ate until I began to read about POLENTA. It turns out that many current and pleasing, ideas about traditional, local foods are more myth than fact; as I have had to realize, the richly laden tables that painters depicted were enjoyed by very few people and the gastronomic abundance of today is a quite recent miracle. Most Italians ate to survive and they ate POLENTA — a sort of mush made of crushed millet or sorghum and water. Very rarely, milk was added and with luck, a bit of oil or old cheese. If there was bread, it was often poorly baked, made from rancid and moldy flour. The citizens of Venice were probably the most fortunate among common people during the Renaissance because their government took great care to keep the city's public granaries full and imposed strict rules for baking and selling bread, but even so, what ordinary Venetians were eating was of no culinary interest whatsoever. However, thanks to a plant discovered in the New World their diet, and that of northern Italians in general, was to change drammatically. This plant was corn, whose history in Italy can be likened to a sort of Cinderella story, set within the Veneto with an extremely happy ending.

Maize, or corn —MAIS in Italian— gets its name from MAHIZ, as this plant was called in Arawakan, the language of the extinct Taino Indians of the West Indies. The word corn, which derives from the old Teutonic KORN, meaning grain, is occasionally used as a general term for all grains, which can create confusion. In Italy there was initially great carelessness regarding the word for corn, perhaps due to a lack of interest in it, as if it did not merit a precise nomenclature. It was called a variety of names, the most common being GRANO TURCO -still used today- but this is a misnomer for corn has nothing to do with Turkey. That country and its inhabitants captured Europeans' fantasies in the 15th and 16th centuries and they imagined that anything new, extravagant or unusual was somehow Turkish. The adjective "Turco" was used indiscriminately for whatever came from foreign, faraway places and thus was given to this strange grain. Likewise, beans from America were originally called FAVE TURCHE and even 'turkey' is an example of this linguistic fashion: that native American bird was named turkey-cock by the British because it resembled cocks, or roosters, and came from an unfamiliar, distant place.

In truth, corn is more mysterious than exotic. Its exact birthplace, whether, Mexico, Central or South America is unknown and it is the only one of all the cereals that does not exist in a wild state; there are many varieties of corn but its wild prototype has never been found and although botanists can trace its hypothetical origins, its evolution remains a secret. This may be because its kernals are too big and heavy to be blown and carried by the wind like lighter seeds or because its tight husk prevents them from escaping:

EAR OF CORN from wooden frieze around Great Door of Palazzo Ducale on the Rio di Palazzo, done during the reign of Doge Francesco Dona (1545-1553) by Scarpagnino (1480-1549). Accessible only by boat + seen well only from the water, this entrance was reserved for Kings, heads of state + other similarly important people. This frieze is proof that corn was known in Venice by 1550 + it may be the first artistic representation of this new plant here.

both features are the result of human intervention in the form of crossbreeding. What is certain, however, is that corn can live only if it is planted and cultivated. It is completely dependent upon people for its survival and, almost as if in recognition of this, it renders a higher yield per acre than any other grain and in some parts of the world, it has been essential for the survival of those who cultivated it.

In March, 1493, when Christopher Columbus returned to Spain from his first voyage to the New

World, corn was one of the things he brought back. It grew in abundance there and the highly civilized Aztec, Maya and Inca Indians worshipped it; indeed, their lives depended on it. Although the early European explorers recognized corn's importance —they called it the "wheat" of the Indians— they did not consider it a food fit for themselves. Nonetheless, some historians presume that Columbus and his men must have willingly eaten roast corn in the West Indies as a welcome alternative to roast iguana. In Europe it was not seen as a source of nourishment but rather, was an object of curiosity, appreciated because exotic. It was planted in the private gardens of dilettante, gentlemen bota-

nists, first in Spain and then elsewhere in Europe, for whom it was of sci-entific interest, a unique specimen to add to their collections of rare plants.

Much of what we know about the presence of corn in Italy we owe to Luigi Messedaglia (1874-1956), a medical doctor from Verona who was also a professor at the University of Padua and a Senator in the Parliament in Rome. His study of the diet and health of the Veneto's rural population and of the terrible disease, pellagra, closely associated with corn, led him to become an expert on the history of this grain and the thoroughness of his research make his scholarly works, published in the 1920's and '30's, relevant even today. Messedaglia called corn "UNA GLORIA VENETA", this glory being due to the fact that it probably was first grown on the island of Murano and its first cultivation in Italy took place within the territory of the Venetian Republic.

Best known for its glassmaking, Murano was once also famous for the splendid summer homes

that Venetian Renaissance Humanists built there, some of whom were interested not only in philosophy and the classics, but in the latest scientific developments as well, and especially in the realm of botany, which was being greatly enriched by the results of the voyages of exploration and discovery then taking place. Virtually all of these villas were more important for their very lush and extensive

FONDAMENTA ANDREA NAVAGERO on Canale San Donato, seen from Canal Grande, Murano

gardens than for their architecture and the most extraordinary one, renowned even outside of the Veneto, belonged to Andrea Navagero (1483-1529). One of Venice's most famous Renaissance humanists, he was a poet, Latin scholar, diplomat and passionate botanist: his garden was celebrated for its amazing variety of rare and wonderful plants, for their beauty and exquisite fragrances and it was very likely the "cradle" of corn in Italy. Navagero represented the SERENISSIMA abroad and was in Seville from July 1524 'til September 1528, then the center for the treasures brought to Spain from the New World. He would certainly have seen corn there and would have obtained some for his beloved garden on Murano, which continued to flourish after his death, tended by faithful friends; none of these gardens still exist. Navagero's official diary described Spanish ships, sailors and society but he also wrote about the flora, fauna, minerals and, not surprising for a Venetian, the fish he saw there. Unfortunately, he died shortly after the end of this mission and was not able to put his notes in order and they remained unknown to scientists; since he was one of the persons most capable of describing plants scientifically at that time, the study of botany was deprived of much valuable information.

Corn was already being cultivated in Spain in the early 1500's and Spaniards probably introduced it into the Campania region in southern Italy where it remained a mere curiosity. The first farming attempts to grow it on Italian soil took place in 1554-5 to the south and west of Venice in Polesine di Rovigo and Villabona nel Veronese, and unknowingly, an agricultural and economic revolution began. Exactly how this came about is not clear; farmers tend to be conservative, diffident, resistent to change, and it would have been quite unusual if the initiative to plant it had come from them. It is possible that some of the Venetians who owned land on the terra ferma knew of Navagero and his knowledge of, and great interest in, botanical developments

FARM MACHINE
hand pulled wooden sower for planting corn. From the Museo della Bonifica (Museum of Land Reclamation) in San Donà di Piave, 50kms. east of Venice

and they encouraged their farmhands to plant this new grain.
Or, maybe they knew of a book such as <u>La preclara narratione
della Nuova Hispagna del Mare Oceano</u> by Hernando Cortés, the
Spanish general who conquered Mexico in 1519. Translated into Italian and printed in Venice in 1524, this work contains several references to
corn, described as being "COMMODA A FAR PANE" — "good for making bread." During the 1500's such books were the main way that Europeans could learn,
and satisfy their curiosity, about the New World, although a few Venetian "Amer-
icanists" corresponded with Spaniards who had been there. But, whatever
the motivating force was, the important thing is that some citizens of the Venetian Republic were willing to experiment and corn's potential was slowly discovered as it moved from elite private gardens to farmers' fields.

By the late 1500's people in the Veneto were eating cornmeal mixed with
other grains to make bread. It was growing on the island of Torcello, in a
few places around Treviso —about 30 kms. from Venice— and in the early 1600's
spread westward into the region of Lombardy. To the east, it grew in the
Friuli region, then part of the Republic, and by 1650, in the province of
Belluno, 100 kms. north of Venice, it had completely replaced all other

BASKET with CORN + GRAPES from
wood sculpture in Sacristy of church
of San Pietro Martire, Murano, which
includes fantastical half-length figures
+ bas-relief panels with scenes from the
life of San Giovanni Battista. They were
done by Pietro Morando for the
Scuola di San Giovanni dei Battuti
from 1652–1656 + transfered to the
Sacristy in 1853 when the Scuola
was demolished.

grains to become people's principal source of nourishment. And, it was cultivated in such great
quantities that it was even exported. One of the most important events in the history of food
was taking place, born in Venice and then nurtured within the region of the Veneto. It
succeeded in producing immediate benefits, such as during the calamitous plague of 1630,
when large amounts of cornmeal were sent to the most severly stricken areas and, with time,
GRANO TURCO would provide much income for the Repubblica Veneta and its citizens. Today,
corn is the primary crop of most of the Po River plain —the PIANURA PADANA— which is one of
Italy's major agricultural areas.

CORNUCOPIAS WITH EARS OF CORN

from monument to Girolamo Cavazza (1588-1680),
a high-ranking government bureaucrat who served the
Serenissima in Italy + Europe. He commissioned
architect Giuseppe Sardi (1624-1699) to design a grand
monument of fine marble + stone for his tomb, + as
testimony of his merits, to stand in the Church of the

Some modern scholars feel that corn's introduction into northern Italy was facilitated by environmental factors rather than by enlightened attitudes towards new plants: the climate and chemical composition of the soil there are particularly well-suited for growing it. In addition to these natural conditions, during the 1600's this area experienced systematic attempts to recuperate land that had deteriorated during the Middle Ages and reclamation and the diverting of waterways succeeded in transforming more than half of what were swamps and sterile terrain into fertile, workable land: much of this was sown with corn. But there is another reason why GRANO TURCO became so important. The Republic had begun its long slow decline, wealth was diminishing and its old practice of buying wheat and other grains was getting too expensive — the solution was corn, whose superiority over the inferior cereals that had replaced wheat centuries earlier was soon obvious. In the 1700's its cultivation spread further south, into the regions of Romagna and Tuscany, and north, into the Piedmont, and corn became the main food of common people, both rural and urban, throughout northern Italy, greatly improving their diet with regard to taste and nutrition. It was no longer just mixed with other grains to make bread: cornmeal began to be used on its own, to make POLENTA.

This new and better food supply was in part responsible for the huge population increase in the Veneto in the late 1600's but corn suffered two stigmas. One was social. POLENTA was considered "poor people's food" and the wealthy did not overcome their disdain for it until the 1800's when, not only did they begin eating it, but they even wrote poems in praise of it. POLENTA thus became fashionable, but it fell out of favor again in the 1800's and became

Madonna dell'Orto. The allegorical statues, putti & large family crest were done by sculptors Francesco Cavrioli (died 1670) & Giusto Le Court (1627-1679). The two cornucopias flank portrait busts of Cavazza's brothers. The work is dated 1654. The church is in Cannaregio.

"acceptable" this time after World War II.

Needless to say, only the rich could indulge in such vagaries of taste. The other, more serious stigma was its association with pellagra, the chronic disease once rampant among northern Italians whose principal food was POLENTA. But, American Indians, for whom corn was equally important, did not get this sickness and it was discovered that they always soaked it in limewater before eating it, which releases its vitamins, and ate other foods like vegetables, beans, meat or fish with it. It was not corn itself which had caused pellagra, but rather, its improper preparation and the lack of a balanced diet, along with unhealthy and backward living conditions. Fortunately, improved nutrition and hygiene have eliminated it.

Corn is often said to be for southern Europe what the potato is for northern Europe but this may be an understatement. Not only food for humans and farm animals, its husks were used to stuff mattresses and because of their slow combustion, cob cores were burned in the little heaters called SCALDINI, used to warm beds in the winter. Today, corn oil is used in cooking, for making soap, in the finishing of leather and as a lubricant.

Considering the amount of POLENTA consumed here every day, one might expect to see ears of corn in Venice's markets but the kernals are nowhere to be seen in Italian cooking. Tourists buy bags of them to feed the pidgeons in Piazza San Marco and supermarkets sell corn for popping but corn-on-the-cob is unheard of as are canned and frozen corn. The size, beauty and color of the kernals are irrelevant since they are ground into meal and flour for POLENTA and a few traditional sweets. The fact that they are reduced into anonymity should not, however, suggest that POLENTA is insipid. On the contrary, it is eaten in a variety of ways —fried, grilled, molded, crunchy, creamy... and is essential to many Venetian dishes: it is part of lots of CICHETI (p.7-11) and accompanies almost every main course, called SECONDI, whether meat, fish or fowl. When other cuisines serve potatoes, rice or bread, Venetians serve yellow or white POLENTA — the color is purely an aesthetic preference for there is no difference in taste. Venetians do not make corn bread and the lack of a characteristic bread is often explained by POLENTA's dominating presence.

I have noticed that foreigners sometimes seem mystified by POLENTA. It comes with the food they ordered but is often left untouched and even people who know exactly what it is think they do not like it. Its appearance is rather unprepossessing so this want of interest is understandable, but it is an unfortunate loss because its neutral flavor truly brings out and enhances a food's taste. For Venetians, however, this behaviour is strange for they cannot imagine eating certain things without POLENTA. In addition to restaurants, it is available in delicatessen-type stores, ready to eat, and there is a packaged, supermarket version, albeit inferior, that needs only to be sliced and heated.

CORN from Delle navigazioni et viaggi by Giovanni Battista Ramusio (1485-1557). Active in Venetian government, he is best remembered for his publications dealing with voyages of exploration & discovery. His 3-volume work, Delle navigazioni, printed in the 1550's in Venice by Tommaso Giunti, is considered the most ambitious geographic book ever produced, significant for its maps as well as it's text. The woodcut of corn was one of the first representations of this new plant which Ramusio described as "...the miraculous + famous corn called maize in the India Oriental on which half the world nourishes itself." Ramusio's closest friend was Andrea Navagero (p.98).

Making POLENTA from scratch requires a strong arm since the cornmeal and water should be stirred constantly for at least forty minutes, always in the same direction. It used to be made daily, in enormous quantities, as "families" could consist of as many as 40 or 50 people and it was usually their main food, and labor-saving devices in the form of POLENTA mixing "machines" were introduced as early as the 1600's. Today, an electric, stove-top version produces excellent results.

"LA POLENTA", painting by Pietro Longhi (1702-1785). It is one of eight canvases depicting "La Vita dei Contadini", or "Peasant Life" done in the mid-1700's. Originally in Palazzo Gambara, on the Grand Canal near the Accademia, it is now in the Museum of 18th century Venice, in Cà Rezzonica

POLENTA

~ 4 SERVINGS ~

13 OZ CORNMEAL ✳

1½ QT. WATER ▶

1 tsp. SALT

✳ Coarsely ground cornmeal makes a more "rustic", chewy POLENTA than the finely ground meal which is better if a softer, creamier POLENTA is called for or preferred.

1) Bring the WATER & SALT to boiling & add the CORN-MEAL. It must be poured slowly & continuously, as if from a very small spout..."A PIOGGIA", rain-like, as Italians say. If it is added too quickly it will form disagreeable clumps & the WATER'S temperature will drop. Lower the heat a bit & begin stirring immediately using a wooden spoon or, if available, a MESCOLA, the traditional instrument used for this, —a cross between a small baseball bat & a slim, round-ended rolling pin. Stir constantly, ALWAYS IN THE SAME DIRECTION, making sure that the CORNMEAL in the lower part of the pot gets incorporated into the upper part. As the POLENTA becomes compact & hard, stirring with both hands may make things easier. A bit of boiling WATER may also be added.

2) After 30-40 minutes the POLENTA will pull away from the sides of the pot, a sign that it is done, but it is recom-mended that the stirring continues for another 20-30 minutes. It is said that POLENTA cannot be overcooked; the longer it is stirred, the better it gets.

3) When the cooking is finished, traditionally the pot was turned over onto a wooden board —rather like unmolding a mold— emptying the contents to produce a steaming yellow mound. Pieces were cut with a string or wire —never with a knife!— & eaten immediately. Today, many people pour the POLENTA into a bowl & serve it with a spoon.

▶ Variations: some of the WATER can be replaced by WHITE WINE, BROTH or MILK, especially when making sweets. (p.172)

The crusty POLENTA that might stick to the bottom of the pot used to be carefully scraped off & fed to chickens even though

it seems children (& probably adults too) loved eating it as a special treat. Soaking the pot in water will loosen it away.

The ways of eating POLENTA seem limitless. It is eaten cold, tepid, hot; with appetizers; with meat, fish and fowl and it is delicious with mush-rooms or with almost any type of cheese melted into it. Leftover POLENTA can be thinly sliced and reheated in the oven, toasted on a grill or fried in oil or butter — the out-side gets a bit crusty while the in-side remains soft. It is even good mashed and put into hot broth.

The rest of this chapter discusses foods normally eaten as the main course, or SECONDO, in Venice which are always served with POLENTA.

FIGÀ A LA VENEXIANA

LIVER VENETIAN STYLE

~ 4 SERVINGS ~

1 LB. VEAL LIVER, cleaned of tissue, sliced as thinly as possible & cut into strips about one inch wide. VEAL LIVER is preferred but PORK LIVER can be used.

1 LB. ONIONS, very thinly sliced

2 TB. OLIVE OIL

2 TB. BUTTER

2-3 TB. fresh minced PARSLEY

SALT & PEPPER

1) Put the OIL, BUTTER & ONIONS in a large skillet & cook over low heat about 30 minutes, until they are very soft & transparent. THEY MUST NOT BROWN. If necessary, add a spoonful of water to keep them moist.

2) Raise the heat to high & add the LIVER. Cook 2 or 3 minutes, stirring. The meat will turn pinkish-brown. Just before turning off the heat, sprinkle it with a dash of SALT & PEPPER & the PARSLEY.

3) Serve immediately, spooning the ONIONS & cooking juices over the LIVER, with POLENTA.

The crucial thing about this recipe is to cook the LIVER very quickly, to keep it from getting tough, which happens if it is overcooked. BUTTER is used, as well as OIL, as it helps keep the LIVER soft; adding the SALT at the last moment also prevents it from getting hard. This dish is normally eaten as soon as it is prepared but it is said to be very good also at room temperature.

BUCRANIUM from EX-MACELLO COMUNALE, the Public Slaughterhouse built in 1843 in Cannaregio by the architects G. Salvadori & G.B. Meduna. It is now part of Cà Foscari, the University of Venice.

Although meat has never been an important part of Venetian cuisine, its history here is not without interest. It is amusing, verging on the incredible, to imagine livestock being raised within Venetian courtyards — a law of 1502 prohibited pigs from grazing in the public squares — and the presence of slaughterhouses seems even more curious considering the quantity of animals such an activity implies and the logistics of getting them there. But goats, cows, calves, sheep and pigs were all part of Venice's gastronomic and economic past, a significant source of tax revenue as well as nourishment. Much of this meat came from port cities in Puglia, Capodistria and Dalmatia but herds of Hungarian cattle came over land as well, driven cowboy-style across the puszta, that country's vast treeless plain, all the way to San Giuliano, just outside Mestre at the eastern-most tip of the terra ferma, where they were transferred onto boats for the two kilometers that separate this point from Venice.

Venice had two public slaughterhouses: one occupied the site of the present fish-market plus the adjoining Campo delle Beccarie and the other, originally on the quay at San Marco, was moved in 1580 to a street near the west end of the Piazza, due to problems created by disagreeable odors and refuse. Later, in the 1600's, butchers were permitted to sell meat in other parts of the city. The word BECCARIA, or meat market, has its roots in the word BECCO, of uncertain but very ancient origin, meaning male goat, or CAPRONE, a meat much eaten during the Middle Ages. The medieval Latin word BECCARIUS, or butcher, gave birth to BECCAIO, both probably based on BECCO, which was eventually replaced with MACELLAIO, meaning slaughtering place as well as butcher. In Venice, until quite recently, the two words were used— MACELLO was the slaughterhouse and BECCARIA, a butcher shop— but today MACELLAIO is the common term for a butcher; animals are no longer slaughtered here.

Documents referring to butchers' stalls near the Rialto Bridge date back to the 11th century and their professional association was founded in the early 1300's. Like other commercial activities the selling of meat was regulated by severe laws designed by the State to protect the public.: butchers who habitually cheated customers over weight, price and/or quality were thrown in the "POZZI", or "wells", the damp, ground floor cells of the Old Prison in Palazzo Ducale, where the most infamous criminals and political went, and were expelled from their profession for three years after they came out.

In the 1800's, for hygienic and sanitary reasons, the Venetian government decided to concentrate all slaughtering in one place on the city's outskirts, and in 1843 the MACELLO COMUNALE was inaugurated, strategically situated facing the mainland and close to the

AMPHORA from 14th cent. well-head in Corte Morosina, San Giovanni Grisostomo, Cannaregio

railroad bridge, begun in 1841; this bridge, built for the train that, then, went all the way to Milan, linked the city of Venice with the terra firma for the first time. The Ponte della Libertà, for cars, built in 1933 was also used for livestock; the MACELLO COMUNALE continued to operate until the 1960's and people still recall the amazing spectacle of scores of animals walking across the lagoon to their fate.

Until fairly recently, only the wealthy ate meat while the vast majority of people could only afford the entrails or MINUZZAME, an old Venetian term for the parts removed from slaughtered meat which includes the head and feet along with the animal's innards. These were sold not by butchers but by LUGANEGHERI: LUGANEGA is a type of pork sausage made in the Veneto and in the Lombardy region, eaten in Venice since at least the 1200's. One of the most popular ways of eating this flavorful sausage was with rice, for RISI E LUGANEGHE, and another favorite, still enjoyed today, is LUGANEGHE with POLENTA (p.111).
In addition to MINUZZAME, sausages and salami, the LUGANEGHERI sold lard and hard boiled eggs, but not fresh ones. Many places in Venice are named LUGANEGHER and reflect the importance that "minute" or "little" meat once had in this city's cuisine.

AMPHORA from 15th cent. well-head in Corte de le Case Nove near Campo de la Lana, Santa Croce

PONTE DEI PENINI

FONDAMENTA DEI PENINI

PENINI is Venetian for PEDUCCI, which are the feet of pigs, goats, lambs & hares. This NIZIOLETO, or street sign, near the Church of San Martino in Castello refers to a shop that sold boiled castrated lambs' feet, or trotters, which was a very common food in Venice until fairly recently.

MERCA
DI RIA

CALLE DE LE BECARIE
O DE LA PANATERIA

SOPA DE TRIPE   TRIPE SOUP

Tripe comes from the walls of a cud-chewing animal's stomach: beef is most common. Each of the stomach's four chambers produces a different quality of tripe; some people use a combination of them, others prefer that of the last three sections: "honeycomb" or DOPPIÒN, omasum or CENTOPELLE — "100 skins", because of its many layers, and abomasum. Venetian butchers sell pre-cooked tripe; if this is not available, prepare it as described below before making this soup.✳ Not surprisingly, calve's tripe is more tender but less tasty than the adult cow's.

~ 4-6 SERVINGS ~

2 LB. BEEF TRIPE✳ cut into thin strips

½ cup OLIVE OIL

2 OZ. LARD cut into small cubes

1 large ONION } chopped
1 stalk CELERY

sprig of ROSEMARY } mince the
2   SAGE leaves   } leaves

SALT & PEPPER

1 BAY LAUREL leaf

1½ QT. boiling BEEF BROTH

toasted BREAD or CROUTONS

6-8 TB. freshly grated PARMESAN CHEESE

1) In a large pot gently heat the OIL with the LARD, ONION, CELERY & the ROSEMARY & SAGE leaves. Cook 'til the ONION is tender & slightly colored.

2) Add the TRIPE, a bit of SALT, the BAY LEAF & enough WATER so that they are covered.

3) Raise the heat to boiling & cook about 2 hours for pre-cooked TRIPE, 3-5 hours for fresh TRIPE. If necessary, add a bit of hot WATER once in a while. At the end of the prescribed cooking time the TRIPE should be tender & there should be very little water left in the pot.

4) Add the BEEF BROTH to the TRIPE. Taste for SALT & PEPPER. Serve very hot with toasted BREAD or CROUTONS & PARMESAN CHEESE.

✳ If the TRIPE is not pre-cooked, it must be rinsed well & left to sit overnight in abundant WATER with ½ of an ONION, a stalk of CELERY, the juice of one LEMON, a few whole PEPPER grains, a sprig of PARSLEY, a sprig of ROSEMARY, 2 BAY LAUREL leaves & 2 SAGE leaves. In the morning, remove the TRIPE, cut it into thin strips & discard the WATER & other ingredients. Proceed with Step 1.

HONEYCOMB TRIPE

CORTE DELLUGANEGHER

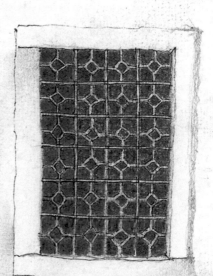

POLENTA E LUGANEGA   **POLENTA & SAUSAGE**

~ 4 SERVINGS ~

4-8 SAUSAGES - pierce them a few times with a
fork, to let their juices out when cooking & cut
them in two lengthwise or in slices ½ inch thick

2½-3 OZ. LARD, finely chopped

(OPTIONAL) 2 TB. dry WHITE WINE

Sally Spector

1) "Melt" the LARD in a frying pan over medium heat.

2) Add the SAUSAGE & sauté it 'til slightly browned all
over. If using the WINE, add it now & cook about 10
minutes. If not, cook about 10 minutes, turning the
LUGANEGA over occasionally.

3) Serve the SAUSAGE, with the cooking juices, immediately,
over hot, creamy POLENTA.

CORTE DEL LUGANEGHER, *between the Frari & Campo San Polo*

OSEI SCAMPAI   SKEWERED MEAT with SAGE

OSEI SCAMPAI means "the birds that got away" and this name is generally interpreted in two ways. One explanation is that the hunting expedition in the lagoon was unsuccessful and thus meat had to substitute for the game birds that did not materialize. The other reason is more ironic: ordinary Venetians ate very few wild birds since hunting was an activity reserved for the wealthy and to make light of their situation, they jokingly contented themselves with bits of liver and meat because their "catch" flew away.

~ 4 SERVINGS ~

3 ¼ oz. CHICKEN LIVERS
  "   "   VEAL or PORK LIVER
} cut into bite-size pieces

6 ½ oz. boneless VEAL
  "   "   PORK LOIN
  "   "   PANCETTA - sliced ¼ inch thick

at least 20 SAGE leaves

~ WOODEN SKEWERS ~

2 TB. BUTTER

SALT & PEPPER

½ cup OLIVE OIL

1 cup dry WHITE WINE

½ cup warm BROTH

1) Heat the BUTTER & sauté the CHICKEN LIVERS in it with a pinch of SALT & 2 SAGE leaves.

2) Thread the MEAT & SAGE leaves on the skewers as follows ▷ a piece of VEAL

SAGE LEAF

a piece of PANCETTA

a piece of CHICKEN LIVER

SAGE LEAF

a piece of PORK

SAGE LEAF

a piece of LIVER

a piece of PANCETTA

SAGE LEAF

3) In a pan large enough to hold all of the prepared skewers, heat the OIL quite hot. Lightly brown all of the skewered MEAT, turning them so that they color all over.

4) Add a bit of SALT & PEPPER & the WINE. When the WINE has almost completely evaporated, lower the heat & add the BROTH, a little at a time, stirring gently. Cook the skewers until the MEAT is tender, about 15 minutes.

5) Serve the OSEI SCAMPAI with their cooking juices over hot, creamy POLENTA.

CASTRADINA

SMOKED LAMB & VEGETABLE SOUP

~4 SERVINGS~

1½ LB. salted, smoked
    castrated LAMB

2-3 CARROTS   }
2 stalks CELERY } thinly
1 large ONION   } sliced

2 medium POTATOES, peeled & cubed

1 green CABBAGE - quartered, then cut
    into thin slices, about 1/8" wide

SALT & PEPPER

1) Rinse the MEAT well in tepid water. Drain it & cut it into medium-sized pieces.

2) In enough WATER so that the MEAT is well-covered, cook it at a medium boil about 45 minutes. The pot should be covered. Remove the LAMB & discard the WATER, which will be greasy & strong smelling.

3) Return the LAMB to the pot with the VEGETABLES. Add WATER until the contents are completely covered & a bit of SALT & PEPPER. Boil slowly, partially covered, for 3 hours or 'til the MEAT is very, very tender.

4) Taste for SALT & PEPPER. Serve the LAMB with the VEGETABLES & a generous amount of the BROTH. This is one of the very few Venetian main courses that does not include POLENTA.

CASTRADINA is the traditional dish eaten on November 21st, the FESTA DELLA SALUTE, or health. In 1630, while Venice was suffering a violent plague that killed almost 50,000 of the city's inhabitants, the Senate voted that when it ended, it would erect a church dedicated to the Madonna as the Protector of Health and that Venetians would visit it every year on November 21st in thanks for the salvation of their city. The famous architect, Baldassare Longhena (1598-1682), designed the church, Santa Maria della Salute. First celebrated in 1681, this ritual still takes place; as in the past, a "bridge" of boats is laid across the Grand Canal from Santa Maria del Giglio to the Salute. Some people still make LA CASTRADINA for the day of the Salute; this meat is not available at other times of the year. It was once quite common during late fall and early winter; poor people ate it often as it was very inexpensive and a filling one-course meal.

SHIP DECORATION wooden sculpture representing sheep wool. During pagan times in the Mediterranean world, when a ship was launched a lamb was sacrificed & its skin was nailed to the prow as a talisman. This tradition continued into modern times but the live animal was replaced by a symbol like this sculpture, which became part of the ship's decoration. Fishermen also adopted this custom in the hope that this "good luck charm" would bring a rich catch of fish. (Naval History Museum, near the Arsenale.)

CHIESA DELLA MADONNA DELLA SALUTE

Birds

For centuries, winged animals and especially game birds were reserved almost exclusively for kings, nobles and the like. Because they could fly and frequent celestial space, these creatures were imbued with symbolic significance denied to terrestrial animals, fish and plants and only the rich and powerful had the privilege of eating them. However, democracy reigned among the earliest inhabitants in the lagoon: the ordinary people who first settled on the islands there found an abundant supply of water fowl and ducks and such birds were among Venetians' "oldest" foods. These included the wild mallard duck, or GERMANO REALE which Venetians call MAZORIN, coots, curlews, geese, guinea hens, partridges, pheasants and quails (FOLAGHE, CHIURLI, OCHE, FARAONE, PERNICI, FAGIANI e QUALIE). Even after Venice was founded and people left the islands in the lagoon for city life, these birds continued to be very present in their diet, whether caught during private hunting expeditions organized for the recreation and amusement of the upper classes or brought by fishermen and those who lived in the lagoon —"islanders"— to sell around the BECCARIE at the Rialto, in Piazza San Marco or in Campo San Polo; chickens and eggs came for the most part from the countryside on the nearby mainland.

AQUATIC BIRD from a 14th century capital of the arcade of Palazzo Ducale. It is thought to represent a bird that no longer lives in the lagoon or that was modified through interbreeding or that may be extinct.

POLASTRO IN SQUAQUACIÒ   YOUNG·CHICKEN·FLOATING·IN·JUICES

The extremely Venetian word SQUAQUACIÒ is considered untranslatable into Italian in the sense that there is no single word that expresses its meaning; a phrase is necessary to get across its significance, which is often the case with dialect words. Although almost all Italian dialects derive from Latin, each one has individual sounds and characteristics that distinguish it from the others and sometimes just one word, all by itself, reveals the essence of these regional tongues. SQUAQUACIÒ is such a word: it generally means "meat in liquid". POLASTRO IN SQUAQUACIÒ is "young chicken floating, or navigating, in TOCIO", that is, in cooking juices. This dish should have a fair amount of rather thick TOCIO, which is soaked up with POLENTA.

~ 4 SERVINGS ~

1 large ONION ⎫ cut
1 stalk CELERY ⎬ into
1 large CARROT ⎪ small
2 cloves GARLIC ⎭ pieces

1 sprig fresh ROSEMARY

2 TB. OLIVE OIL
2 TB. BUTTER

SALT + PEPPER

3 LB young CHICKEN,
   cut into 6-8 pieces

½ cup WHITE WINE

1 small can TOMATOES

1) Cook the ONION, CELERY, CARROT & GARLIC with the ROSEMARY in the OIL & BUTTER over medium heat until slightly softened but not browned.

2) Add the CHICKEN with a bit of SALT + PEPPER.

3) Cook gently about 15 minutes, stirring occasionally. Raise the heat + add the WINE. When it has reduced a bit, add the TOMATOES with their juice, mashing them gently. Cook a minute or two, mixing all the ingredients together well.

4) Lower the heat, cover + cook slowly about one hour.

5) Serve with POLENTA.

ROOSTER+HENS from mosaic decoration in the Atrium of the Basilica di San Marco depicting the story of Noah, west side of vault, south of main entrance: "Noah Bringing Fowl into the Ark", 13th cent.

Venice's poultry vendors, the GALINERI, were divided into two distinct groups: the POLLAROLI sold both domestic fowl and wild aquatic birds while the BUTIRRANTI sold fresh eggs and butter - light goods that were easy to carry around. As with all other trades, the government imposed strict laws on the GALINERI: the POLLAROLI had to clearly display their birds in cages or baskets and they had to sell them personally, not through middlemen; the BUTIRRANTI could not accumulate and store their eggs, nor hide them overnight in shops or bars, but had to sell them absolutely fresh, as a law regarding this stated, "from one Avemaria to the next", referring to the traditional three strikes of the bell known as L'AVEMARIA which rang at dawn and evening every day. A leniency clause, however, permitted the BUTIRRANTI from Chioggia to keep their eggs overnight in their boats, to be sold the next day. The GALINERI were CONTADINI, peasants from the countryside, often looked down upon by Venetians who considered them "picturesque". They were notorious for their lively, noisy ways and legendary shrewdness and it seems that it was often difficult to enforce the laws that were supposed to regulate their commerce.

EGG MERCHANT in
Campo Santa Margherita, Dorsoduro

Today, duck and game birds are less present in Venetian cuisine than in the past. During the hunting season people catch them and poultry shops and butchers offer them, but chicken is the most common fowl eaten nowadays. All domestic chickens descend from the wild species *Gallus gallus*; they originated in southeast Asia, were introduced into Egypt and Greece during the Persian Wars in the 5th century B.C., then spread throughout Europe and are now found across the globe. Venetians, and many Italians, consider chickens from the area around Padua, about 30 kms. west of Venice, to be the best available, and indeed, the GALLINA PADOVANA is one of the four most famous species in Italy; known since antiquity, it is prized for its delicate taste.

In addition to being a source of nourishment, wild birds had an important place in Venice's history in the form of OSELE. The OSELA was merely a coin, a small thin disc of silver or gold, but its significance went far beyond its physical aspect for it represented the Doge and his rôle as head of the Venetian State. While initially the Doge had almost absolute power, as the Venetian government developed and defined itself, his sovereignty was reduced until he was only a figurehead: the Doge reigned but he did not govern. However, he did have a few special rights and particular privileges; for example, certain hunting areas were reserved for his own personal use, the best one being in the lagoon of Marano, about 70 kms. east of Venice. Game was highly valued and in 1268 it was decreed that every December 4th, the Doge had to give wild ducks and birds caught in his private game reserves to all those who had helped him attain his high position, such as members of the Great Council and high ranking officials. These gifts were called OSELE, which is the Venetian word for birds; in Italian it is UCCELLI, from the Latin word AVICELLUM.

The most prized OSELA was the mallard duck, called MAZORIN, and the female was considered more tasty than the male.

OSELA minted by Doge Francesco Erizzo. It shows a tree in full bloom, flanked by two heads representing wind; above the tree, the Madonna holds the child. Around the border are the words DEDI SUAVITATEM ODORIS, which allude to the terrible plague that ended in 1630 & proclaim that Venice's air was once again clean & healthy thanks to the grace of the Virgin.

The Doge's obligation became increasingly difficult to fulfill due to climatic changes — a long period of declining temperatures in Europe during the Middle Ages reduced the number of MAZORINI in the lagoon — and an increase in the number of Great Council members. The birds were replaced by a gift of money but this did not please the recipients and thus it was decided to mint a special coin every year in the Doge's name, to be called an OSELA, to symbolize the original

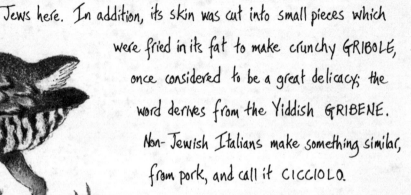

RED-LEGGED PARTRIDGE detail from the painting "The Annunciation" by Tiziano (1490-1576) in the Scuola di San Rocco. This European fowl was one of the most prized game birds in the lagoon.

offering of wild birds. From 1521 until the end of the Republic in 1797, the OSELA was issued each December bearing the Doge's name, sometimes preceded by MUNUS, meaning gift. The same coin, or variations of it, was normally repeated during successive years of a Doge's reign, with a change of date; the images were usually of religious, political or patriotic significance.

Goose is another fowl that was present in Venetian cuisine into the 20th century, well after the OSELE were no longer minted. Much of Venice's Jewish population was of Central European origin, from Bohemia, Hungary, Austria and Germany. They did not use olive oil, as did Mediterranean Jews, and when preparing a meal that included beef or lamb, used goose or chicken fat; Jewish dietary laws prohibit cooking such meat with butter or milk products, nor should these two types of food be digested at the same time. More than chicken fat, Venetian Jews used goose, and this bird was also used for making liver paté, sausages and salami which enjoyed a certain fame even among non-Jews here. In addition, its skin was cut into small pieces which were fried in its fat to make crunchy GRIBOLE, once considered to be a great delicacy; the word derives from the Yiddish GRIBENE.

Non-Jewish Italians make something similar, from pork, and call it CICCIOLO.

CURLEW detail from altarpiece "Virgin Enthroned Adoring the Child" (1450) by Antonio da Negroponte in the church of San Francesco della Vigna, Castello.

Sally Spector

PONTE NOVO,
RIO DI SANT'ANNA, CASTELLO

Sally Spector

Fish ~ Pesce

Fishing is, if not the most ancient, certainly one of the oldest ways of earning a living in the Venetian lagoon. Ever since it was inhabited, —recent archaeological research shows settlements dating back some 2,000 years— people have been catching the great variety of fish, mollusks and crustaceans that fill these waters. It is thanks to this marine life that the lagoon is also rich in aquatic birds which eat the fish. The move from the original island communities to what would become the city of Venice, which began in the 9th century, created a distinction between "urban" and "rural" work: those who remained in the lagoon were mostly farmers and fishermen while city life encouraged the development of artisan trades and commerce.

Venice's population did include fishermen, or PESCATORI —from the Latin word PISCES, meaning fish (etymologists theorize than an Indo-European word, PISK, may be the source for both PISCES and fish); some lived in Cannaregio, the north-west part of Venice, but most were near the Church of San Nicolò dei Mendicoli, at the south-east edge of the city. Originally right on the lagoon, now separated from it by modern construction, this was a rather poor area as even the church's name suggests: MENDICOLI is Venetian for MENDICANTI, or beggars and Saint Nicholas is the patron saint of all seamen because he supposedly tamed ferocious waves that threatened to wreck his boat while sailing to the Holy Land. However, the vast majority of fishermen were on Giudecca, Torcello, Murano, Mazzorbo, Poveglia, Burano, Pellestrina and Chioggia and, to this day, fishing is still an important livelihood in the last three of those places. Unlike other occupations, there was no apprentice period for PESCATORI; sons went out with their fathers from a very early age and learned how to cope with bad weather and dense fog, and to face danger as fearlessly as possible, in addition to the art of fishing. Their lives and working conditions have greatly improved in the last decades, thanks to the introduction of motors, which replaced oars and sails, radar and nylon fishing nets; in the past, much time was spent repairing broken cotton nets but nylon is much stronger and thus now there are more days that can be devoted to fishing.

The lagoon consists of various types of fishing environments such as the open sea, the shoreline and the "interior." This last one is characterized by enclosed expanses of water called VALLI DA PESCA, or "fishing valleys," which are surrounded by areas of barely emerged land, called BARENE, that are submerged when the tide is high; the VALLI are like little lakes or big ponds within the larger lagoon. The floor of these distinct zones may be sand, mud or gravel; their depths vary from shallow to several meters and depending on their configuration and where they are, they experience the ebb and flow of the tide every six hours with differing intensity. In addition, they are inhabited by different kinds of fish caught by various techniques from suitably diverse boats.

PESCA DA POSTA "TRESSA" These are seen in many parts of the lagoon, used mostly for catching eel, cuttlefish & goby. Nets are tied to wooden stakes that are inserted into the lagoon's muddy floor, arranged perpendicular to water currents which carry the fish through the circular openings into the "COGOLO" at the end, from where they cannot get out.

The jurisdiction of this landscape was a primary concern for the Republic. Land, even if swampy, could be privately owned, but the lagoon's waters belonged to everyone although the VALLI DA PESCA, which were like fish hatcheries, could be leased from the State. The natural changes and variations inherent in a lagoon ambient, in the delicate balance between land and water, called for constant vigilance. Special authorities were established to protect, control and prevent abuse of this precious resource from erosion by the sea, the silting up of rivers, pre-industrial pollution and unlawful possession or usurpation. The Venetian government realized that no one understood the ways and character of the lagoon as thoroughly as did fishermen and in 1536, decreed that eight of the oldest and wisest of them were to participate in the COLLEGIO LAGUNARUM when this area was discussed.

Red Goatfish
(p.132)

TRIGLIA DI FANGO barbon fam. Mullidae, Mullus barbatus

Sally Spector

The lagoon's physical environment was not its only aspect that was carefully watched: the State also safeguarded the life it contained as a benefit for all Venetians and in the interests of fishermen. Fish nets had to be of a specified weave, loose enough so that tiny baby fish would not be caught and were left free to grow. During certain months some types of fishing gear were prohibited, some types of fish could not be caught and some areas were totally off-limits. The minimum size of fish that could be sold was also stipulated and incised on stone tablets: an example still hangs at the Rialto Market.

Like other commerce in Venice, the selling of fish was highly regulated and was divided into three categories. The PESCATORI had to bring their catch to the Rialto where, every day, the quality of their fish was controlled, they paid duties, and prices were determined; as with other essential foods, the government set a maximum selling price, called CALMIERE, in order to prevent speculation. The second group, called COMPRAVENDI, or "buyer-sellers", were wholesale fish merchants who could sell only at the main markets at the Rialto and San Marco; this was quite lucrative work, restricted to those who were at least 60 years old and who had been fishermen for at least 20 consecutive years. The PESCIVENDOLI, the retail fishmongers, could sell at the main markets as well as in other parts of the city. All fish vendors had to sell their goods completely in the open —no shops, no roofs over their heads— and all fish had to be completely visible. But, in spite of laws, regulations and penalties for fraudulent behavior, a certain amount of illegal commerce took place; for example, sailors on the ships anchored in the Bacino near San Marco would often sell fish in the Campo San Giovanni in Bragora, not far from there, and various ruses to make old fish look fresh were common.

PESCATORE by Giovanni Grevenbroch (1731-1807) from Gli abiti de' Veneziani di quasi ogni età con diligenza raccolti e dipinti nel secolo XVIII. (the clothes of Venetians of almost all ages, gathered & painted with diligence in the 18th century) Very little is known about this Venetian artist of Flemish origin, best remembered for his 4 volumes of watercolors representing all aspects of Venetian life in the 1700's: political & religious figures, professions, artisans, manual laborers, merchants etc. along with unusual events such as the presence of a rhinoceros in 1750. These 648 watercolors were commissioned by Grevenbroch's noble patron, Pietro Gradenigo, + are all accompanied by a page of text, often of a rather curious, sometimes comical character. The comments for this fisherman refer to this profession's legendary tendencies to deceive & cheat their customers..."It is supposed that those who did so had to keep one bare foot in a bucket of cold water during the winter + were prevented from wearing a cap in summer to protect them from the heat of the sun... but they are robust + such punishment does not keep them from filling their purses." These works are a valuable source

SallySpector

of information regarding 18th century Venetian clothes + accessories while those depicting typical jobs such as cleaning canals or implanting the tall wooden stakes for marking canals + mooring boats, called PALI, are like "photographs" of this city's past.

Preparing & Eating Fish

Venetians prepare fish and seafood very simply and quite quickly. Frozen fish is now available here but the catch of the day is always preferred, usually fried, grilled or stewed although it may be steamed or boiled, depending on its type, size and the season. The animal's pure, natural taste is not masked or modified by sauces or spices...no mayonnaise, no cheese, no stuffing and baking: nothing interferes with or overpowers the fish's characteristic flavor and taste. Fish are normally served whole with the head and tail which some foreigners do not like. If this is a problem, in a restaurant one can ask that they be removed before the fish is served.

For frying, vegetable oil is used, not olive. If, as might be imagined, economic factors determined this choice in the past —vegetable oil is much cheaper— one could expect this to change today, but the neutral vegetable oil continues to be preferred: olive oil is considered too strong, too heavy for the delicacy of seafood. Venetians do not deep-fry their fish; they use just enough oil for the animal to be almost submerged and it must be very, very hot so it cooks as quickly as possible to absorb as little oil as possible. Vegetable oil maintains a high temperature better than olive, which also makes it preferable. Fish are always lightly dusted with flour just before being fried, a method regarded as an art because the true expert knows exactly when to flour, when to put them in the hot oil and when to remove them. Once fried, they are always immediately set on absorbent paper to eliminate any exterior oil and eaten hot, perhaps sprinkled with salt, pepper and lemon juice. Sardines are an exception: they are often fried —whole or head removed, split open, butterfly-style— and eaten hours later at room temperature as CICHETI (p.7-11). Venetians call them "PESCI AZZURRI", or "blue fish", as they call certain small fish from the northern Adriatic; their high fat content keeps them from drying out as much as leaner "PESCI BIANCHI", or white fish, which are dry and tasteless if eaten cold. The numerous types of quite small fish that abound in the lagoon area are usually eaten fried and are often included with the shrimp and cuttlefish in Venice's justly famous FRITTO MISTO DELL'ADRIATICO, or "fried-Adriatic-seafood-mix".

Although it is always preferable to grill fish over hot coals, it may not be possible ; some people get very good results with a small electric pan. The fish is usually seasoned with a bit of olive oil, lemon juice, salt and pepper. While restaurants serve the FRITTO MISTO in a single portion, the GRIGLIATA MISTA is prepared for a minimum of two... the larger the order, the more variety there is and Venetians often order it family-style, with everyone sharing the various fish that may be included such as angler, bass, brill, eel, gilt head, mullet, plaice, St. Peter's fish, sardine, sole etc.... (RANA PESCATRICE, BRANZINO, ROMBO, ANGUILLA, ORATA, CEFALO, PASSERA, SAN PIERO, SARDINA, SOGLIOLA) all of which are also eaten on their own, as an individual serving.

Stewing, IN UMIDO or, as Venetians say, CO'L TOCIO, is usually limited to cod, cuttlefish and eel. While fried and grilled fish are also served with POLENTA, the juice, or TOCIO, that stewing produces makes the cornmeal a greater delight than usual, in addition to being absolutely necessary. SEPE CO'L TOCIO NERO, cuttlefish stewed in its black ink, is one of the most "VENEZIANI" of all dishes (p.141); BISATO IN UMIDO, eel stewed with bay leaf, is equally divine. Without POLENTA, they are incomplete.

The lagoon is also rich in mollusks and crustaceans which find their perfect habitat in its sandy, muddy environment. A few of them, like the razor clam and the mantis shrimp are not often seen else-where and are well worth trying. The following is a list of the various fish and seafood found in Venice with a brief physical description to help recognize them. Almost none of these creatures lives within the lagoon for the whole year. Rather, they migrate from there to the nearby shores of the Adriatic. Most of the females lay their eggs in the sea during the winter and return to the lagoon in early spring and many fish go to the sea in late September, when the lagoon's waters start getting cold, and stay there until the spring when they warm up.

Angler RANA PESCATRICE/ CODA DI ROSPO   coa de rospo   fam. Lophiidae, Lophius piscatrius

The big head, wide mouth and strong teeth of this black fish give it an extremely menacing look. The angler lures its prey by means of a sharp, threadlike growth on its head that its victims believe is food but is, instead, a weapon with which they are "fished" and snapped into its mouth — thus its name RANA PESCATRICE, or "frog-fisher." Its tasty, large-flaked white flesh is usually grilled; the meat of its "tail" is especially prized and gives it the name Venetians use — CODA DA ROSPO, meaning bullfrog's tail.

Bass BRANZINO/SPIGOLA   branzin/baicolo   fam. Serranidae, Dicentrarchus labrax

Many people judge this Venice's most delectable fish. It can be as long as one meter but is normally half that and is grilled when small, baked or boiled when large. The Venetian word BAICOLO refers to the BRANZINO up to 12 months old; a famous Venetian cookie created in the 1700's is called BAICOLO (p.178) because its oval form resembles this young fish.

Brill ROMBO   rombo/soàsa   fam. Scophthalmidae, Psetta maxima / Scophthalmus rhombus

There are two types of this rhomboid form flatfish in the lagoon: ROMBO CHIODATO and ROMBO LISCIO. The first is darker, named for the black spots on its dorsal resembling nails, or CHIODI; since it is the biggest of the flatfish, reaching up to a meter long, fishermen call it the "King" of the muddy lagoon floor which is the only place it lives. The second is less tasty and thus cheaper, but since it can be mistaken for the CHIODATO, in spite of its lighter color, it is sometimes sold for more than its worth.

FOSSENA or FOSSINA (FIOCINA in Italian)

This forked iron instrument usually has 8 or 10 sharp prongs & a wooden handle. Slight variations in its design adapt it for catching mostly brill, eel & plaice.

SOTOPORTEGO
DEI D...

Sally Specter

Eel ANGUILLA bisato

fam. Anguillidae, Anguilla anguilla

While this fish has six different names depending on its length, Venetians just call it BISATO. The lagoon's brackish water and muddy floor are its preferred habitat and many live in the VALLI DA PESCA. It is eaten all year round: when small, it is fried, medium length ones are grilled and the biggest – females can be over a meter long – are stewed. Extremely nutricious, eel is also very fatty, making it hard to digest, but highly recommended all the same.

SOTOPORTEGO DEI BISATI

This covered passageway leads to the Zattere & the Canale della Giudecca. It is in Campo Sant' Agnese, near the Church of the Gesuati, where eels were once sold, called BISATI by the Venetians.

BISATO SULL'ARA Murano's glass makers discovered an additional function for one of the ovens used in their work: they made BISATO SULL'ARA. For them, ARA, which was the sacrificial altar for the ancient Romans (+ also signifies a large rooster + an area measuring 100 sq. mts.) is a particular stone that has the quality of absorbing a great deal of heat. Once a piece of glass is made, its temperature must gradually decrease from that of the oven to the exterior environment's, + to facilitate this process it was placed on the ARA. Glass workers used to put a whole eel, wrapped in heavy grease-proof paper with just a few bay leaves, on the hot ARA + it would slowly cook in its own fat. This was traditional on the day before Christmas but it was also made at other times during the year, shared among all the workers. BISATO SULL'ARA is no longer made.

Gilt Head ORATA orà/orada   fam. Sparidae, Sparus auratus

This elongated-oval shaped fish is one of the lagoon's most prized; its name in both English and Italian comes from the bright orange to gold markings on its head and the bright strip of gold between its eyes which become more pronounced with age. It prefers the deep water around the lagoon's BARENE although it comes to the surface where fishermen easily recognize it, due to its extraordinarily beautiful and elegant swimming style. Its tasty white meat is usually grilled. A close relation is the PAGELLO, or bream, called PAGELLO FRAGOLINO by Venetians because of its reddish-pink coloring — FRAGOLA is strawberry.

Goby GHIOZZO gò   fam. Gobiidae, Gobius ophicephalus (p. 145)

Of the four types of small goby fish found in abundance in the lagoon, Gò is by far the most present in Venetian cuisine. Since swampy environments with algae are its natural habitat, fishermen call it one of the "FIGLI", or children, "DELLA LAGUNA". The female does not lay her eggs in the sea; instead, when the lagoon's waters begin to get cold, she digs a hole that becomes a U-shaped den under its muddy floor and deposits her eggs. She then departs, leaving the male to watch and protect the thousands of potential GÒ. Dark, with black, marble-like markings and spots, it is usually eaten fried, in fish soup or for RISOTTO.

Mackerel SGOMBRO scombro   fam. Scomberidi, Scomber scombrus

This PESCE AZZURRO rarely enters the lagoon; rather, it stays about 50 meters from the shoreline, in large schools —it never swims alone— which come to the water's surface at dawn and just after dusk. Its very delicate meat is usually grilled; its high fat content means that, like the sardine, it is also good cold, as a CICHETO (p. 7-11).

Gray Mullet CEFALO bosega   fam. Mugilidae, Mugil chelo

Of the five types of mullet in the lagoon, the BOSEGA is considered by far the best and is a great favorite of Venetians. It is usually grilled or boiled. Like the BRANZINO, the baby CEFALO is called BAICOLO.

Sally Specter

THE BAKER *from the sculpture cycle of the "Trades"
on the Great Arch of the Basilica di San Marco framing the main entrance to the Church, dated early 14th cent. The baker, seated
on a wooden bench hands a young woman two small loaves of bread which she pays for with two fish. Two young apprentices
stand behind them, each one holding a basket of bread. The one on the left, with the basket on his head, suggests one of the
more incredible things one sees in Venice today: teen-age boys carrying large trays of baked goods which they balance on
their heads, walking with perfect equilibrium — up & down bridges — with their hands in their pockets.*

Mullet/Goatfish TRIGLIA barbon fam. Mullidae, Mullus barbatus/Mullus surmuletus

There are two types of TRIGLIA in the lagoon. TRIGLIA DI FANGO, or mud, is reddish pink with two thick hairlike growths, or BARBIGLI, on its lower jaw; this organ of touch is the source for its name in Venetian. The TRIGLIA DI SCOGLIO, or rocks, called TRIA in Venetian, is larger, reddish orange with two barbels and is much more prized and more expensive. But, since it can be difficult to tell them apart, BARBON is sometimes sold at the price of TRIA. When small, they are fried, when big, grilled.

Sole SOGLIOLA sfògio   fam. Soleidae, Solea vulgaris Quesnel

The light grayish-green tones of this flatfish's dorsal camouflage it on the lagoon's sandy bottom, as well as in the VALLI DA PESCA and in the sea. Sole is said to be the best of the "mud-floor dwellers" and is very expensive. There are three other types of sole in the lagoon, good but not as good as the vulgaris. Two of them are much darker, almost black (Solea lascaris Risso and Solea Kleini Risso), so it is easy to recognize them but the third, the SOGLIOLA ADRIATICA (Solea impar Bennet), is light colored; it can be identified by a sort of pore close to its mouth —its name in Venetian is PORÀTO— but nonetheless, it is often sold as SFOGIO. All of these fish are eaten fried, grilled or steamed.

Saint Peter's Fish SAN PIETRO sampiero fam. Zeidae, Zeus faber

Also called John Dory, this silver-olive-gray fish has long dorsal spines, a large mouth and a dark round spot on both sides of its compressed, oval body which, according to some, appeared after Peter, the patron saint of fishermen, removed a coin from its mouth to pay a tax. But, the fishermen in the lagoon have a different explanation: once, after fishing all night, Peter finally caught one fish. He was so angry that he grabbed it from the net and flung it into his boat, leaving his fingerprints where he had grasped the fish. Since then, all SAMPIERI have these marks, which are one of its most distinguishing characteristics; another is that after being caught, its gills emit a strange, low, groaning sound. It is among Venice's most prized white fish and is rather expensive. It is usually eaten grilled.

Tuna   TONNO *ton*   fam. Thunnidae, Thunnus, thynnus

Adriatic tuna is smaller than that of the Atlantic or Pacific. It is famous for its VENTRESCA, or the meat from its belly, which is high in fat, and for its eggs, called BOTTARGA which are dried and salted. Fresh tuna is usually grilled or stewed; the VENTRESCA is sold loose, by weight from large tins and found in many grocery stores.

Saint Peter's Fish

SAN PIETRO

sampiero

SARDELE IN SAOR are eaten all year round; often included among CICHETI offerings, they are also served as a main course, and it is traditional to have them on the third Saturday of July, on the eve of the FESTA DEL REDENTORE. Perhaps Venice's most celebrated holiday today, this festival is a wonderful mix of the spiritual and the temporal: on Sunday, a holy visit to the Church of the Redeemer, or REDENTORE, on the Giudecca, and spectacular fireworks on Saturday night which Venetians watch from boats of all sorts and sizes, gaily decorated with paper lanterns, candles etc., anchored in the BACINO — the "basin" of water between San Marco and the Island of San Giorgio Maggiore. Hundreds of people gather there in the early evening and eat elaborate picnic dinners while waiting for the nearly one hour show of fireworks that starts around 10:30.

SARDELE IN SAOR is one of Venice's "oldest" dishes, still extremely popular today, made of lightly fried sardines and onions marinated in vinegar and salt for at least 24 hours (p.137); many people recommend 48 hours of marinating and its taste gets even better after that. Marinating fish to preserve it goes back at least to the ancient Romans. For them, as for the Venetians, it was an important food for fishermen and sailors who could keep it on board ship for days and sometimes weeks. In this recipe, the salt, vinegar and onions conserve the fish and since onions are rich in vitamin C, this dish was useful for preventing scurvy, the disease that seamen were once so vulnerable to. During the winter months, thanks to Venice's trade with the Eastern Mediterranean, pine nuts and raisins were added; their extra calories made it more nutricious and filling and thus helped one withstand the cold better. Those ingredients are rarely included today.

The bridge on the right is PONTE DEI LUSTRAFERRI, named for the iron polishers who once had a shop there. The other, longer bridge is PONTE DELL'ASEO, or vinegar - ACE in Italian— named for the vinegar "factory" that, in the 14+1500's, st the CALLE DELL'ASEO that connects That wine turns into vinegar has perha since that drink was first made: vin ferred to in the old Testament as "w + Roman soldiers drank it diluted wit their thirst during long periods of marchin sons for this transformation were not u

vinegar was considered mysterious
while it was clear that air facilitated the process, not until the
French chemist, Antoine Lavoisier
(1743-94) discovered oxygen was the
acidifying mechanism explained. Then,
in 1864, another French chemist, Louis
Pasteur, (1822-95) showed that a certain bacteria called
MYCODERMA ACETI was necessary for converting alcohol into
acetic acid & the industrial production of vinegar was born.

There is another CALLE in Venice named ASEO, near Campo
Santa Margherita in Dorsoduro; it is thought to be the name of a
family that once lived there & has nothing to do with vinegar.

The FESTA DEL REDENTORE commemorates the ending of a plague that broke out in Italy in 1575; an exceptionally dry, hot summer made it particularly fierce in Venice and the Doge, in the name of the Senate, vowed that a church would be built, when it ended, dedicated to the Redeemer, and that the Doge would make an official visit there every year in thanks for Venice's salvation. The plague was declared over in July, 1577: a temporary tabernacle was immediately erected on the site chosen for the new votive temple, on the Giudecca, and a "bridge" of boats was arranged, stretching all the way from the Doges' Palace to this shrine, decorated with a series of trellised archways for the Doge and his procession. The architect Andrea Palladio (1508-1580) was commissioned to build the Redentore; he died before it was finished but his precise directions regarding construction techniques, measurements and building materials were scrupulously followed.

At first, this holiday was strictly religious but with time, Venetians added the joyous and bacchanalian to the devotional and REDENTORE remains an important weekend here, celebrated by natives and visitors alike. The bridge of boats no longer extends from Palazzo Ducale, for there is no Doge, but rather, from the Zattere, on the opposite of the Giudecca Canal facing the Church. A pontoon bridge is laid by the Italian army which, for two days each year, allows one to walk the 300-some meters over water that is normally traversed only by boat: crossing this wide canal on foot is an extraordinary experience. In the past, after the fireworks, some people would go to the Lido to wait for the sunrise on the beach. It is interesting to note that no one remembers it ever having rained on REDENTORE...

Sardine   SARDINA   sardela

fam Clupeidae, Sardina pilchardus Walbaum

The lagoon's sardines are actually from just outside its three openings to the Adriatic; they rarely enter the lagoon. They live in large schools in the lower half of the sea but always swim to its surface at dawn & dusk. The fishermen of Chioggia & Pellestrina were experts at catching this fish; older people there remember when — before the use of motors — as many as 25 boats would set out four hours before the sardines' punctual arrival, their orange sails making the procession a true spectacle. Adriatic sardines are particularly flavorful & very inexpensive. Venetians eat them fried, grilled & in SAOR; they almost never eat them tinned. They are consumed both as CICHETI (p.7-11) & for the main course, accompanied by POLENTA.

SARDELE IN SAOR

"SAVORY" SARDINES

2 LB. small fresh SARDINES, scaled & cleaned. Heads & tails may be left on or removed.

2 LB ONIONS, very thinly sliced

FLOUR for Step 2 below

VEGETABLE OIL - for frying the SARDINES. Venetians do not fry fish in OLIVE OIL as its taste would overpower the fish.

Proportions are for an equal amount of SARDINES & ONIONS. Two pounds of each will serve six people as a main course. Leftovers can be kept for quite a while in the refrigerator.

SALT - PEPPER

1/2 - 3/4 CUP WHITE WINE VINEGAR

4 whole BAY LEAVES

CONTAINER - glass or earthenware - for marinating: A four-sided, deep form is better than round & shallow because more layers help keep the food more moist.

1) Rinse the SARDINES in cold water. Drain them well or dry them with paper towels.

2) Dip the fish in FLOUR, dusting them lightly so they are completely covered.

3) Cover the bottom of a skillet with OIL, using as little as possible. Heat it & fry the fish but NOT TOO MUCH. They should remain soft, almost as if boiled & not get stiff & crusty. As soon as they are fried, while still hot, sprinkle them with a bit of SALT. Let them cool while the ONIONS are prepared.

4) In the past, the ONIONS were cooked in the same OIL used for frying the SARDINES — OIL was very precious & reused whenever possible. Today it is felt that this OIL, although certainly very tasty, would be too "fishy", too strong & maybe difficult to digest & it is discarded — fresh oil is used, but as a compromise, a bit of it can be kept, mixed with the new. Once again, just cover the bottom of the pan with a veil of OIL. Add the ONIONS, VINEGAR, BAY LEAVES & a dash of SALT & PEPPER & cook very gently for 45 minutes or until the ONIONS are withered. Keep the pan covered but stir occasionally.

5) Cover the bottom of the container with a thin layer of ONIONS. Arrange a layer of SARDINES over them, then another layer of ONIONS, alternating them until they are all used. Be sure that the top layer is ONIONS. The 4 BAY LEAVES can be placed over them as decoration.

6) The SARDINES must marinate at least 24 hours; they get better after 48 hours & continue to improve. It is best to marinate at room temperature. This dish can be kept in the refrigerator but it must be eaten at room temperature, never chilled.

7) Serve the SARDINES and ONIONS accompanied by warm or cold POLENTA.

Mollusks   Molluschi

Clam   VONGOLA VERACE caparozzolo   fam. Veneridae, Tapes decussatus

Of the different clams that live in the lagoon, the most acclaimed is
the VERACE, recognized by its nearly circular form and its beige-brown
coloring with brownish-black speckled markings. Its tasty meat, almost
sweet, is eaten raw, with lemon juice or cooked, in RISOTTO or with SPAGHETTI.

Murex   MURICE garusolo fam. Muricidae, Murex trunculus / Murex brandaris

There are two types of this one-valved mollusk in the lagoon area: the female trunculus
is greyish-pink with brown ribbing, has a slightly rounded form with projecting bumps
and ridges and lives in the lagoon, while the tastier male brandaris is yellowish-gray, more
slender and elongated, with sharper projecting spines and lives in the sea. They are boiled and
eaten cold, as a CICHETO (p. 7-11).

Mussel   COZZA peocio fam. Mytilidae, Mytilus galloprovincialis

The natural habitat of this violet-black, triangular-shaped bivalve is along the banks of canals and on
the rocks at the three port openings between the lagoon and the sea. They live in large clusters, held
together by their BISSO, or byssus, the strong silk-like filaments some mollusks use for attaching onto
something, which is the source for their name in Venetian: PEOCIO, meaning louse –PIDOCCHIO in Italian–
comes from the fact that they cling, like lice, to rocks and BRICOLE, which are the tree trunks
marking the lagoon's canals, and are usually arranged in groups of three.

Razor Clam   CANNOLICCHIO capa longa   fam. Solenidae, Solen siliquosa / Solen vagina

The two main types of these long, slim bivalves found in the area around Venice are the siliquosa,
which lives in the lagoon and the vagina, which inhabits the sea. Their shells are yellowish-
white with tones of beige and pink; a large "foot" extends from the front end and the intestines
from the other. Both are edible, but the siliquosa is used mostly as bait; the vagina is a true gastronomic

treat —almost sweet— usually sauteed and eaten as an ANTIPASTO. Venetians also call these clams CAPE DA DEO, or DITO, meaning "finger mollusks", from the way they can be caught. CAPE LONGHE live deep down in the sand along the shoreline, burrowed in a vertical position. When the tide is low, their presence is recognized by a tiny air bubble, the size of a pin head, visible on the surface of the sand. By thrusting a finger down below this bubble to block the clam's movement, it is possible to pull the animal up out from the sand.

VI   G

SOLEN VERO MAS from an engraving in De Conchis Minus Notis (regarding lesser-known shells) by Giovanni Bianchi (Janus Plancus) (1693-1775). Born in Rimini, Bianchi studied medicine at the University of Bologna + was a professor of anatomy at the University of Siena. While the lagoon's plant life was studied as early as the 1500's, De Conchis, written in Latin + published in Venice in 1739 by Giovanni Battista Pasquali, was one of the first books to deal with its fauna + even includes the barnacles that inhabit Venice's canals. Bianchi left numerous writings, mostly on anatomy + teratology. His works also discuss the port of Rimini, extol the art of comedy + consider whether a vegetarian diet is beneficial for the health + for curing certain sicknesses.

Scallop CAPPASANTA capasanta
fam. Pectinidae, Pecten jacobaeus

Like the CAPA LONGA, the fan-shaped, deeply ribbed CAPA SANTA lives deep down in the sand. One of the lagoon's tastiest and most prized mollusks, it is usually SCOTTATA, or scalded, in a pan with a bit of oil, garlic, lemon juice, parsley and salt —the heat makes the shells open— or it is baked.

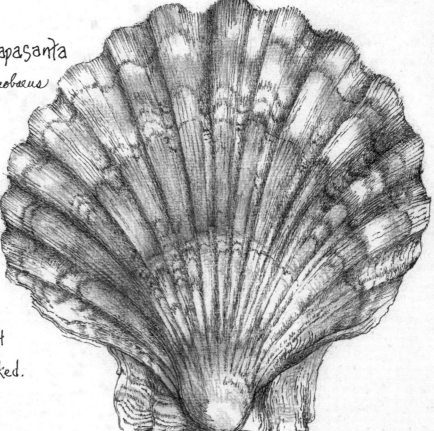

Octopus   POLPO   folpo   fam. Octopodidae, Octopus vulgaris Lama

The opening of this cephalopod's sac-like body is its mouth, surrounded by eight tentacles equipped with suckers. Although it can get quite large —even three meters long— it is best young and small, which is how Venetians eat it. It lives in the cracks and fissures of rocks and scientific research shows it is the most intelligent of all invertebrates, with highly developed brain cells. Its gray color turns pink-violet when cooked; usually stewed or boiled and marinated, it is eaten as a CICHETO (p.71) or in salads.

Small Octopus   MOSCARDINO   moscardin   fam. Octopodidae, Eledone aldrovandii - Rafinesque

MOSCARDINO is the Italian word for a type of dormouse as well as the name of this relative of the FOLPO and derives from MUSCHIO, or moss. It is very small —about 25 cm.— and although it is called "white" octopus; it is much darker than the vulgaris. Varying from gray to yellow, mottled with dark green, it blends in with fragmented rocks and the sandy lagoon floor where it lives. Its very tender, flavorful meat is best boiled, fried or eaten in salads.

Cuttlefish   SEPPIA   sepa   fam. Sepiidae, Sepia officinalis

In spite of their name, cuttlefish are mollusks, not fish, thus part of the 125,000 species of invertebrate animals that make up this group whose origins date back a million years. The term mollusk derives from the Latin MOLLUSCA, a soft-shelled nut; it refers to the soft, bag-like body of these creatures, usually covered by a hard, very often beautiful, exterior shell which, in the case of the cuttlefish, was transformed by adaptive evolution into a single interior supporting bone or spine. Cuttlefish, along with octopi and squid make up the highest order of mollusks, called Cephalopods, from two Greek words of Indo-European origin —KEPHALE and PODO meaning head and foot, because their head is encircled by their numerous tentacles which are used for locomotion, as if they were feet. "Cuttle" comes from old Teutonic, meaning bag or pocket. The SEPIE in the lagoon have a short, oval body; their internal bone is very hard and flat and they have ten tentacles with suckers, two of which are much longer than the others. Except for these tentacles, they are quite different from squid or calamari which have an elongated, slightly tapered body with a thin, pen-like interior spine. Cuttlefish respond to external stimuli with psycho-chromatic reactions: when they sense danger, they change color and become covered with spots that move, combine, separate and change in size, which also camouflage them when hunting food or to escape being eaten by dolphins, sharks or cormorants. To defend themselves, they expel their ink, blackening the water around them so their enemies cannot see them, used in this recipe....

SEPE IN UMIDO col TECIO NERO   CUTTLEFISH STEWED IN ITS INK
~ 4 SERVINGS ~

2 LB. CUTTLEFISH   OLIVE OIL   2 cloves GARLIC, left whole

½ cup dry WHITE WINE   SALT & PEPPER   2-3 TB. minced fresh PARSLEY

1) Wash the SEPE in cold water. Remove the eyes with a sharp knife. A scissor is recommended for the following: cut off the TENTACLES & the mouth with the hard part around it. Keep the TENTACLES. Remove the internal "bone"— pushing on the end opposite the mouth helps slide it out. Cut the body open lengthwise, taking care not to pierce the tiny, silvery INK SAC. With a sharp knife, gently detach the SAC & set aside. Remove the entrails & discard them. Under running water, pull off the very thin outer skin: it will be smooth & white underneath. Cut the SEPE & TENTACLES into small or medium-sized pieces, as preferred. Put them in a colander to drain.

2) Cover the bottom of a large pot with a veil of OIL, put in the GARLIC & cook over medium heat. When the GARLIC starts to brown, remove it. Put in the SEPE, TENTACLES, INK SACS, WINE, a dash of SALT & PEPPER & the PARSLEY. Stir well, breaking the INK SACS. The mixture will become black.

3) Cover the pot, bring to a boil & lower the heat. Cook very slowly, covered, about 40 minutes or 'til tender. Stir once in a while. The contents will be quite liquidy, as the SEPE release water as they cook; to thicken, uncover towards the end of the cooking to let some of the moisture evaporate.

4) Serve with POLENTA. This dish is good reheated, or leftovers can be used to make **RISOTTO DE SEPE**, as follows: Remove the pieces of SEPE & heat the liquid to boiling. Add RICE, stir well & cook a few minutes. Add simmering WATER, a bit at a time, as for a RISOTTO (p. 62) maintaining a boil & stirring constantly. After about 15 minutes, mix in the SEPE & continue to cook, stirring, until the RICE is done.

It was once believed that SEPE are an aphrodisiac due to the complex, sensual

intertwining of their tentacles when copulating, but today they are eaten mostly for their exquisite texture & taste.

Crustaceans   Crostacei

Crab GRANCHIO granzo (m.) masaneta (f.) fam. Cancridi, Carcinus maenas

This small crab, from about 1½-3 inches in diameter lives on the lagoon's sandy floor and in the brackish water near the mouths of its rivers, as well as near its three openings into the sea. Its dark brownish-green shell turns bright red when boiled; its meat is seasoned with oil, garlic and parsley. The female is considered more tasty than the male, fishermen distinguish them by their differently shaped abdomens. While these crabs are good, they are far less prized than the MOLECA.

Soft-Shelled Crab GRANCHIO moleca fam. Cancridi, Carcinus maenas

When the GRANCHIO has grown too big for its shell, sheds it and is waiting for a new one to form, it becomes a famous Venetian delicacy — a MOLECA, or soft-shelled crab... MOLLE means soft in Italian. MOLECHE are available only in April, May, September and October. They are lightly floured and fried; some people put them first in beaten egg which the live crab soaks up and then fry them, which gives them an almost fluffy quality. The entire animal is eaten, legs and all, and seems to melt in one's mouth.

CANCER the CRAB from Clock Tower in Piazza San Marco. This clock was made by Carlo & Paolo Ranieri in the late 1490's; it shows the hour, movement of the sun, signs of the zodiac, phases of the moon & principal constellations. Its mechanism still functions.

Spider Crab GRANCEOLA granzon (m.) granzeola (f.) fam. Majdae, Maja squinado-Herbst

Long-legged, with a very rough, knobby, reddish shell from 6 to 8 inches in diameter, this "Queen" of crustaceans lives deep down in the mud and sand. It provides one of Venice's most elegant appetizers: the GRANCEOLA is boiled —live, like the GRANCHIO— and its meat is finely chopped, along with that of its two large pinchers, seasoned with lemon juice, a bit of oil, salt and pepper, and served cold in the animal's shell. The GRANZEOLA's CORALLO, her mass of immature, fertilized red eggs is often mixed in with her white meat, creating a visual effect equaled by its taste.

Mantis Shrimp CANOCCHIA / CICALA DI MARE / PANNOCHIA   canocia
fam. *Squillidae, Squilla mantis*

The CANOCIA lives on the lagoon's muddy floor. It has projecting, stalk-like eyes and a fan-shaped tail fin with two dark spots in its center; its long, segmented body is the basis for its being called PANNOCHIA, meaning a spike of grain or "ear" of corn, and CANOCCHIA, from CANNA, meaning cane or rod. While it is as long as four, and even six, inches, its sweet meat is a minor part of it compared to its elaborate, intricate shell. Usually boiled, CANOCIE are a favorite appetizer, seasoned with a squeeze of lemon.

Gray Shrimp GAMBERO GRIGIO   schila   fam. *Crangonidae, Crangon vulgaris*

This shrimp is so tiny —about one inch long— that its stalk-like eyes and short beak are quite difficult to see; its grey color turns pink when cooked. Once eaten mostly by poor people, disdained by the wealthy perhaps because of its diminutive size, as were other of the lagoon's small creatures, SCHILE are now considered a delicacy. They are usually fried: the whole animal is eaten, shell and all, and served with grilled POLENTA, as an appetizer.

WOODEN BOAT used for fishing in the lagoon: the bucket held the fish that were caught; from a scale model in the Museo Storico Navale, near the Arsenale. In 1778, the Arsenale founded a school for training draughtsmen, builders + modellists + that school created most of the scale models in the Museum's collection today.

BACALÀ MANTECATO ~6 SERVINGS~ CREAMED SALT COD

2 LB. BACALÀ, soaked ✳

1 clove GARLIC

OLIVE OIL - as necessary

SALT & PEPPER

1) Put the FISH in a pot, cover with cold WATER & bring to a boil; skim off any foam that forms on the WATER's surface. When it reaches a full boil, turn off heat & let sit for 20 minutes.

2) Pound the GARLIC to a paste with a mortar & pestle.

3) Drain the FISH, remove its skin & open it to bone it. Put it in a sturdy container & break its flesh into tiny crumb-like pieces with a fork. Slowly pour OIL into the FISH & vigorously beat them together. As the BACALÀ absorbs the oil the mixture should become very frothy; the amount of OIL necessary depends on how lean or fat the FISH is.

4) Stir in the GARLIC & a dash of SALT & PEPPER. Serve with slices of warm grilled POLENTA.

The word BACALÀ, meaning SALT COD, probably derives from the Spanish word for fresh cod – BACALAO – which may come from the old Dutch word for it: BAKELJAUW; it is dried in the open air & preserved with salt. BACALÀ was introduced to the Mediterranean by the 15th century Venetian explorer & navigator, Pietro Querini, whose account of his nordic voyage was included in Ramusio's Delle navigationi (p.102): in January, 1432, Querini & his crew were shipwrecked on a reef near the Lofoten Islands off Norway's northwest coast & a few days later were rescued by fishermen from Røst, a nearby island, where they stayed 'til May. The area was rich in but one thing: codfish; the only other fish there was plaice. Querini described how the natives dried the cod in the sun & wind; as it was very lean, it became very hard & they would beat it with hatchet handles to soften it for eating. More than just food, this preserved fish was that people's only source of income & they traded it in northern Europe for such things as iron, wood & cloth. Querini, who had never seen it before, likened it to "minted coin" in "unlimited amounts" & when he & his men left for Venice in the spring, they took this preserved fish with them. Initially eaten mainly by Germans living in Italy, Italians began consuming it in the 1600's. These two recipes are among the most popular ways to prepare it.

BACALÀ A LA VICENTINA ~6 SERVINGS~ SALT COD 'ALLA' VICENZA"

2 LB. BACALÀ, soaked ✳

3 TB. FLOUR

4 cloves GARLIC } minced
2-3 TB. fresh PARSLEY

3/4 cup plus a few drops, OLIVE OIL

SALT & PEPPER

1 medium ONION, chopped

1 QT. MILK

3¼ OZ. freshly grated PARMESAN CHEESE

4-5 ANCHOVY fillets, chopped

1) Cut the FISH in small pieces & dip them in the FLOUR.

2) In a large pan, gently cook the GARLIC & PARSLEY in 3/4 cup OIL 'til the GARLIC is soft. Remove half of the mixture & set aside. Add the FISH to the pan & cook slowly 'til it starts to color. Sprinkle with a dash of SALT & PEPPER, add the ONION, cover with the MILK & bring to a boil.

3) Lower to simmering & cook slowly 'til the MILK is almost all absorbed.

4) Stir in the CHEESE & ANCHOVIES & sprinkle with the GARLIC-PARSLEY mixture. Pour a few drops of OIL over the FISH & cook for about 10 minutes in a moderate oven (325-350°).

5) Serve hot with POLENTA.

✳ Soaked BACALÀ is sold in ALIMENTARI, or small grocery stores & by some fishmongers.

~ This is a rare example of a dish eaten in Venice made with FISH & CHEESE. ~

SOPA de PESSE

FISH SOUP

Considering the variety of and differences among Italy's regional cuisines, and this country's more than 7,000 kms. of coastline, it seems natural that there is not one classic Italian fish soup but, rather, countless variations on this theme; merely within the lagoon there is diversity, not to mention just the northern Adriatic area. In addition to geographical factors — where, within the Mediterranean, the soup is made — its contents also used to depend on the time of year but today fish are imported to Venice from all over the world so such considerations are less relevant.

Goby
(p.130)

~ 6 SERVINGS ~

4 LB. FISH - a variety of different types is best. The choice depends on what is available & within one's means: fishermen's families normally used whatever fish were left unsold from the day's catch. BASS, COD, SQUID, CUTTLEFISH, EEL, MACKEREL & SHRIMP are good but any firm-fleshed seafood is suitable.

1 LB. MUSSELS - remove their "beard" & scrub off exterior sand & dirt

2 medium CARROTS } chopped
2 stalks CELERY

2 QT. WATER

2 BAY LAUREL leaves

SALT & PEPPER

½ cup OLIVE OIL

1 medium ONION } finely chopped
2 cloves GARLIC

½ cup WINE VINEGAR

3 ripe TOMATOES, peeled & chopped

toasted BREAD or CROUTONS

1) Wash & scale the FISH. Remove their intestines & discard them. Cut off their HEADS TAILS & FINS & bone them & set them aside for the BROTH. Cut the meat into medium-sized pieces & set aside.

2) Put the CARROTS & CELERY in a pot with 1½ QT. WATER, BAY leaves, a dash of SALT & PEPPER & the FISH HEADS, TAILS, FINS & BONES. Bring to a boil & boil slowly about 20 minutes.

3) In another large pot cook the OIL with the ONION & GARLIC 'til the ONION is soft & transparent.

4) Add ½ glass of WATER & any shellfish except the MUSSELS to the ONION & GARLIC. Cook gently about 10 minutes. Add the cut-up FISH & cook a few more minutes, stirring gently. Add the VINEGAR & when it has evaporated, add the TOMATOES.

5) Strain the FISH BROTH, pressing the ingredients with a spoon to extract their juices & add the liquid to the FISH & TOMATOES, with a dash of PEPPER. Boil very slowly about 20-25 minutes.

6) Add the MUSSELS & boil slowly another 5 minutes.

7) Taste for SALT & PEPPER & serve with toasted BREAD or CROUTONS.

FRUIT & VEGETABLE BOAT
This green-grocer is also a
farmer, from Tre-Porti, who
brings his boat from there,
laden with fruit, vegetables
& fresh flowers to three
different places each week:
two days in Santa Croce, two
days in Murano & two days
in the spot shown here, on
the FONDAMENTA DEI ORMESINI,
in Cannaregio, where he can
be found every Tuesday &
Friday morning.

148

Vegetables   Verdure

Archaeological evidence shows that people have inhabited the lagoon since prehistoric times and its agricultural history dates to a similarly distant past although information becomes more precise with Roman settlements, some 2,000 years ago. The Romans planted grapes and vegetables and continued the ancient practice of bringing flocks of sheep to graze there because its salty grass offers the sodium these animals need: still today, one occasionally sees a shepherd herding scores of them across the highway just outside Venice to the shores of the lagoon. The farming presently carried out in this area owes its origins to the "first" Venetians, the inhabitants of the nearby mainland who fled such cities as Altino, Padua and Treviso when northern European tribes crossed over the alps and invaded them in the 5th century.

These refugees found safety in the lagoon but they also found an environment very different from what they were used to. The lagoon's marshy "islands" are barely above sea level; the tide rises and falls an average of 40 to 100 centimeters every twelve hours and high tides often cover the lowest areas, called BARENE. The water is salty and the soil is sandy. Winter temperatures rarely go much below freezing but the bora, the fierce cold wind that blows from over the mountains to the north-east, can severly damage spring crops. With time, however, the "islanders" learned how to deal with these difficult conditions. Their success, in which the vast gardens of the lagoon's once numerous monasteries and convents played an important part, resulted in a thriving agriculture and turned what initially were liabilities into benefits: the chilly winter temperatures are often moderated by gentling sea breezes, making it possible to produce very tender, often precocious vegetables known as PRIMIZIE, and the sandy soil and salty environment create a slightly bitter taste, highly prized, for example, in the tiny artichokes called CASTRAURE (p.156) which are a delicacy unique to the lagoon.

There are three agricultural zones in the lagoon: SANT'ERASMO, CHIOGGIA and CAVALLINO-TREPORTI. They all have a similar soil composition —sandy, with little humus, they are relatively close to

The abundance & high quality of the produce available in Venice during the 15th & 16th centuries were described by foreigners & Venetians alike. This quote from Marin Sanudo (1466-1536) is an example:

Par a Rialto un horto, tante erba da li
lochi vicini portate vi viene et tante et varij
frutti et bon mercado, che è cossa mirabele.

(The Rialto seems like a garden, so many vegetables are
brought there from nearby places and such quantities and
varieties of fruit, at such low prices, that it is miraculous.)

A participant in his city's political life, Sanudo is best remembered for I Diarii, the 58 volume Diary in which he wrote on nearly all aspects of the SERENISSIMA, from transcribing official documents to details of ordinary, everyday Venetian life.

each other and benefit from the warming effect that a large body of water has on temperature, but each one has a distinct micro-climate. Cavallino-Treporti, just north and east of Venice, are closest to the sea and most exposed to the bora; severely hit by the terrible flood of 1966, today their agriculture is almost entirely a green-house one. Chioggia, at the lagoon's southernmost tip, is also on the sea, but its farms are located on the interior, towards the west, and are thus less vulnerable to frigid north winds. Sant' Erasmo is the most favored of the three, for it lies entirely within the lagoon; the waters' thermal influence is greatest there and Cavallino-Treporti help cushion it against the bora, which in the past was also blocked by the groves of Mediterranean sea-pine trees that once grew along the shore.

Much of Venice's produce still comes from the farms in the lagoon, as it has for centuries, although some changes have occurred: one of these involves transport. In the past, the farmers who got to the market at the Rialto first had the best chance of selling their crops and thus they would set off in the night, rowing or sailing across the lagoon by moonlight, sleeping in their boats, in order to arrive by dawn. They did this all year long, through fog, wind and rain until the 1950's, when motors began to replace oars and sails which significantly shortened the trip and reduced its dangers. Other changes include the introduction of heavy farm machinery, fertilizers, insecticides and irrigation, but perhaps the most profound ones have been the development of large-scale 'industrial' agriculture and trucking, Italy's membership in the European Economic Community and the relatively recent growth of supermarkets, to which Italians have been more resistent than other Europeans. As a result, there is now a much greater variety of foods to choose from and the time of year no longer necessarily determines what there is to eat.

During my first years in Venice, in the mid-1980's, I would pass the Rialto Market every morning and I began to understand the intimate relationship between the time of year and the produce available which had not been evident in the big North American cities I had lived in 'til then. All of a sudden, the stands were full of bright green pea pods and then, from one day to the next, they disappeared until the following year. And the same thing happened with asparagus and string beans, cherries and tiny gold plums. Venice's greengrocers, or FRUTTIVENDOLI, are like a living calendar: their beautiful stands sign the passing of the months as the seasons change and they are stunning proof of people's ability to cope with, and adapt to, their environment. Unfortunately, many of Venice's small grocery stores have disappeared, not always ousted by the supermarket phenomenon but instead, often victims of the city's declining population and its ever-increasing tourist industry that caters more to visitors than residents. The remaining FRUTTIVENDOLI still offer much local produce, usually identified by hand written signs saying SANT'ERASMO, CHIOGGIA, CAVALLINO or VIGNOLE, another place in the lagoon devoted to agriculture.

Much of the Venetians' creativity regarding vegetables is expressed in the rice dishes this city is famous for but there are, all the same, a few typical CONTORNI or side dishes... CONTORNO means contour, something that frames, embellishes, garnishes. Their preparation is extremely simple: boiled, steamed, sauteed, stewed or grilled and served with just a bit of oil or a squeeze of lemon — no sauce, no cheese, no cream. Cooked vegetables are normally eaten at room temperature which often upsets foreigners who wrongly interpret this cold food as a sign of carelessness or disrespect —Venetians do not expect their soup to be as hot as foreigners want it, either. From a North American point of view, these vegetables can seem overcooked, and at first I was critical, but have come to find that while the longer cooking may indeed mean a loss of vitamins, it is greatly compensated for by their fuller, wonderful taste.

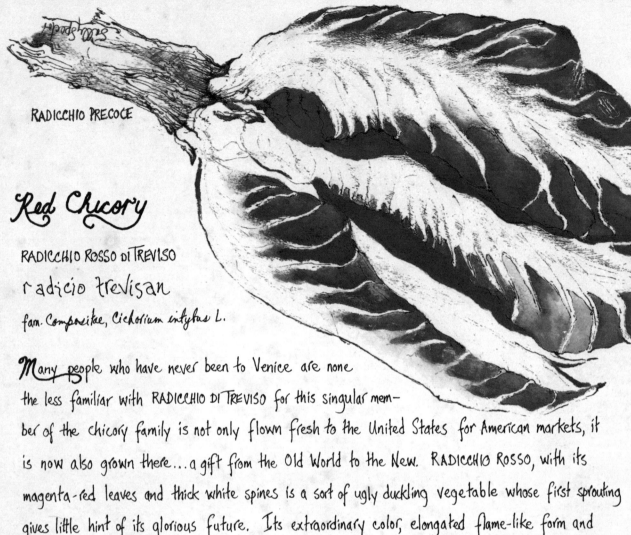

RADICCHIO PRECOCE

Red Chicory

RADICCHIO ROSSO DI TREVISO

radicio trevisan

fam. Compositae, Cichorium intybus L.

Many people who have never been to Venice are none
the less familiar with RADICCHIO DI TREVISO for this singular mem-
ber of the chicory family is not only flown fresh to the United States for American markets, it
is now also grown there…a gift from the Old World to the New. RADICCHIO ROSSO, with its
magenta-red leaves and thick white spines is a sort of ugly duckling vegetable whose first sprouting
gives little hint of its glorious future. Its extraordinary color, elongated flame-like form and
robust, handle-like root were developed and perfected by human intervention but this red lettuce
is prized for more than its aesthetic qualities; the sweetness of its leaves combined with their
slightly bitter spine create an unusual, distinctive taste and even its texture is notable — the leaves
are delicate, soft and tender while the spine is meaty and crunchy. The plant's root, or RADICE,
which gives RADICCHIO its name, is discarded but some people recall that when food was less
plentiful than today, it too was eaten.

Radicchio Rosso is generally believed to be the creation of Frank Van Den Borre, a Belgian
botanist who, in 1860, moved to Preganziol, a small town near Treviso, about 30 kms. from Venice.
His experience with Belgian agricultural techniques for modifying plants — Belgian white endive is
perhaps the best known example— led him, in the late 1800's, to experiment with this chicory

using methods that both forced and accellerated the development of its internal leaves. This is acknowledged as being a very refined salad leaf and it may be amusing to note that until the 1950's both the initial germinating period and the very delicate final phase of its cultivation required plentiful supplies of fresh cow manure.

Around Treviso, RADICCHIO seeds are planted with the first full moon of July. In the past, they were then covered with a thick layer of manure to help them grow strong roots that would push as deeply into that area's clayish soil as possible; today, chemical fertilizers are used. A long, strong root is essential for this plant: it is said that farmers can tell how healthy the RADICCHIO's root is just by looking at its leaves. It needs little attention until the first frost, usually in November, at which time from 15 to 20 individual plants are gathered into a big bunch, like a large bouquet of flowers, and intensive treatment begins

These bunches used to be "replanted" in large quantaties of fresh cow manure for about eight days, which kept them warm, moist and out of the light. During this time the outer leaves withered or were removed, while the inner ones deepened to their full red color and the bitter taste reached its maximum. Here too, the traditional cow manure has succumbed to modern hygienic standards and economics, and farmers are now saved the labor and fatigue of maintaining a store of natural fertilizer, made expensive and difficult by the fact that they keep fewer cows today: the manure has been replaced by a hydro-technique. Now, the RADICCHIO bouquets are kept in cement tubs in a dark environment while warm water constantly flows around them, using a process

SPADONE or RADICCHIO TARDIVO

that works faster than the old manure method. Some people feel that the RADICCHIO's taste has suffered from these changes, but whether this true, or just nostalgia for the past, is hard to say.

There are two types of RADICCHIO DI TREVISO – PRECOCE, or early, and TARDIVO, or late, easily identified by the form of their leaves. The precocious is available from September through November; its leaves are wide, open and flower-like but, in spite of its greater beauty, it is considered less of a delicacy than the TARDIVO, whose season goes from about the 20th of November to early March. Late RADICCHIO is also called SPADONE, from the word SPADA, meaning sword, because of its spear-like form. Its leaves are darker red but almost non-existent, over-taken by their thick white spine, flame-like and curved at the tip. This is the most prized of all salad leaves and has brought fame and fortune to the city and province of Treviso, whose name it bears.

On the Saturday before Christmas the city of Treviso hosts its annual RADICCHIO fair: both an exhibition and beauty contest, it has taken place every year since 1889 – not even two World Wars stopped it. Farmers present baskets of their prized red chicory outside the Palazzo dei Trecento in the Piazza dei Signori, and first and second prizes are awarded for color, proportion, beauty of the leaves and root size. In recent years, neighboring areas have inaugurated similar fairs in the interest of maintaining RADICCHIO's excellence. Related varieties are the RADICCHIO DI CASTELFRANCO, DI CHIOGGIA and DI VERONA, all within the region of the Veneto. Rounder in form and less intense in color, they lack the flavor and texture of the RADICIO TREVISAN.

There are currently many recipes using RADICCHIO ROSSO and new ways of using it are constantly being created. Venetians sometimes make RISOTTO DI RADICCHIO, in which the red leaves are chopped and cooked with the SOFFRITTO and the rice takes on a dark, reddish-brown color. Grilling it is also common but many people claim this vegetable is best eaten raw, like lettuce, seasoned with olive oil, vinegar and salt. Purists, however, eliminate the oil and vinegar and do nothing but sprinkle it with a bit of salt.

Artichoke CARCIOFO articioco   fam. Compositae, Cynara scolymus

Both the English word artichoke and the French word ARTICHAUT come from the Italian CARCIOFO which is believed to derive from the Arab name for this vegetable: al-HARŠUF. The Venetian word is easy for English speakers: ARTICIOCO. Native to the Canary Islands and the Mediterranean area — they need a dry, mild climate — artichokes probably descend from the thistle. These two plants closely resemble each other and share the same bright violet-blue flower but the vegetable must be picked before it blossoms; otherwise, it becomes inedible.

The ancient Greeks and Romans were quite fond of artichokes but they were not cultivated in the lagoon until the 1500's. Today they are grown in most parts of central and southern Italy and in northern Italy, those of Liguria and the Veneto are particularly delicious: they are among the most prized crops harvested in the lagoon. These artichokes are different from other Italian types in that they are generally longer and thinner with regard to bulb and stem, their leaves are pointed but not menacingly sharp, and their green coloring

has a striking magenta-violet cast which is why they are often called CARCIOFI VIOLETTI DI CHIOGGIA.

More unusual, however, than their physical beauty is the fact that their soft, internal part, the "heart", is completely edible: there are no unpleasant stringy or "furry" parts. Unfortunately, many visitors here do not know this and often leave what they think is the choke, uneaten, thus missing a real treat.

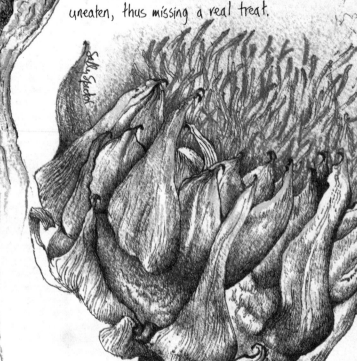

In Venice, artichokes are often boiled or steamed and eaten in the usual way, pulling the leaves out and biting their "meat" off until one gets to the best part, in the center. But, there is another way that they are eaten which dispenses with the stem and leaves and goes directly to the "heart" or bottom – the FONDO, as it is called here. Many produce stands have basins with whitish, disk-like forms, about two inches in diameter, floating in them: they are FONDI DE ARTICIOCHI. Vegetable vendors, usually men, slice off the artichoke's leaves and stem with artistic mastery to produce this delicacy which is eaten steamed, grilled or fried.

Another Venetian specialty is the CARCIOFINO or CASTRAURA, the baby artichoke whose name derives from botanical "castration", in which the stamens are removed from a plant's flower. These come mostly from Sant' Erasmo, where farmers cut off the first shoots from the artichoke's main stalk, leaving only three or four, so that the plant has fewer offspring to nourish and each one gets a bigger share of food. Available for only a short time and rather expensive, these new-borns are appreciated for their slightly bitter taste due to the salty earth they grow in. They are easily recognized: miniature artichokes with a purple tinge and a slim stem whose elongated, wavy leaves frame them like a fluttering, open collar.

Culpepper's Complete Herbal, printed in London in 1654, claims that artichokes provoke lust. This may, or may not, be true but in any case, Venetians used to eat them for another reason. They ate the local CARCIOFINI raw, dipping their tender leaves in olive oil seasoned with salt and pepper "PAR GUARSE EL DENTE", meaning "in order to grind (clean) the teeth", to prepare their palate for the next course. The chemical reaction that artichokes produce in the mouth does, in fact, make certain foods taste better, or at least different.

FONDI DE ARTICIOCHI   ARTICHOKE BOTTOMS
~ 4 SERVINGS ~

8 FONDI - they are sold by the number, not by weight

c. 3 TB. OLIVE OIL

2 cloves GARLIC, left whole or finely minced
  Some people like the taste of GARLIC and mince it
  for this dish; others cook the cloves whole just to
  flavor the OIL + discard them before cooking the FONDI.

2-3 TB. fresh PARSLEY, finely chopped

SALT - PEPPER

1) Cook the GARLIC very gently in the OLIVE OIL
   in a shallow pan large enough to hold all the
   FONDI in one layer. THE GARLIC MUST NOT BURN.
   If discarding it, do so as soon as it begins to color.

2) Arrange the FONDI in the pan; they may touch
   each other but should not overlap. Sprinkle
   them with the PARSLEY + a bit of SALT + PEPPER.

3) Cover + cook slowly about 10-15 minutes, until
   tender. Check occasionally + add a few drops of
   WATER if necessary. They are done when a fork pierces
   them easily. They should not get mushy.

4) They are often eaten at room temperature but
   are also good slightly warm. Serve with a
   spoonful of their cooking liquid.

Uncooked FONDI should be kept in water with a
few drops of vinegar or lemon to prevent them from
turning black.

FONDI are eaten both as a CICHETO (p.7-11) + as
a vegetable side dish, or CONTORNO.

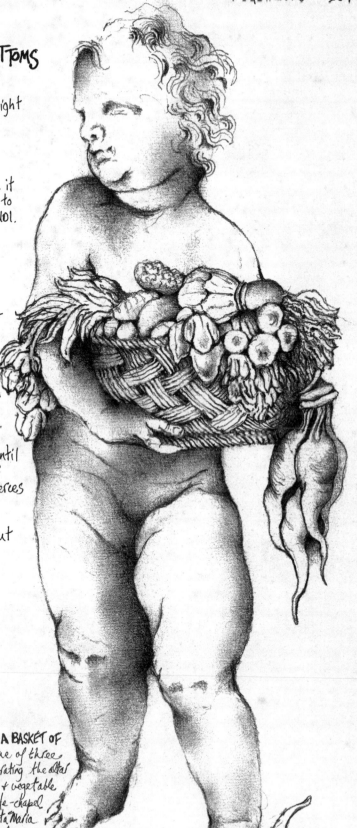

PUTTO HOLDING A BASKET OF
VEGETABLES - one of three
statues decorating the altar
of the fruit + vegetable
vendors in a side-chapel
in the Church of Santa Maria
Formosa, Castello. Dated circa
1600, the sculptor is not known.

FONDI DE ARTICIOCHI

Cabbage   CAVOLO VERZA/CAPUZZO   fam. Cruciferae, Brassica Sabauda/Brassica oleracea

Cabbage originated in the Mediterranean and is now cultivated in many parts of the world. Its Italian name, CAVOLO, comes from the Greek word KAULOS and the Latin CAULUM, meaning stalk or caulis. The medieval French word CABOCHE, meaning head, from CAPUT -Latin for head- may be the source for the word cabbage. In the ancient world, the Greeks used it as a remedy for drunkeness while the Romans recognized its beneficial effects on digestion and were generally very fond of it. The great Roman military officer and writer, Pliny the Elder (23-79 A.D.), mentioned five different varieties of it in Naturalis historia, the 37 volume encyclopedia he wrote on the natural world which includes anthropology, astronomy, botany, geography, medicine, minerology, zoology etc.

As with other foods in Italy, the same type of cabbage has different names in different regions and even within Venice, these terms can sometimes create confusion: broccoli and brussel sprouts, for example, are often called CAVOLO. The most common varieties here are VERZA or CAVOLO VERZA and CAPPUCCIO, CAPUZZO in Venetian. The former is Savoy cabbage, with dark green leaves which are wavy and crinkly, almost as if "blistered," with an occasional dark purple tinge, open, exposing the head. The latter, lighter green cabbage, has smooth leaves that wrap tightly around it. CAPPUCCIO, as in the coffee-milk drink called CAPPUCCINO and the Capuchin monastic order, means hood, while VERZA probably derives from the Latin word VIRIDIS, meaning green.

FARM IMPLEMENTS- from collection of models of old farm machines + tools, Dept. of Agriculture, University of Padua, (p. 61)

Local cabbage is available almost all year long: VERZA is in season from October to January and CAPPUCCIO from May to October. This plant was once a very important food, especially for poor people; whether in spite of or because of this, 'CAVOLO' is often used idiomatically to refer to something of little value, as in "NON VALE UN CAVOLO" -"its not worth anything" or, "it's not worth a cabbage."

VERZE SOFEGAE   "SUFFOCATED" CABBAGE
~4 SERVINGS~

2 TB. OLIVE OIL   2 cloves GARLIC, minced or chopped   sprig of fresh ROSEMARY

2 lb. GREEN CABBAGE, finely sliced, not grated   SALT   PEPPER

1) In a large pot gently heat the OIL + GARLIC with the ROSEMARY. The GARLIC should not brown.

2) Add the CABBAGE. Raise the heat a bit + stir the CABBAGE. When it starts to wilt, lower the heat + add a dash of SALT + PEPPER.

3) Cover the pot + cook very, very slowly for 2-3 hours. The CABBAGE "suffocates" + reduces to about 1/3 of its original volume.

4) Serve warm or at room temperature.

It is worth making this in a fairly large quantity because it keeps well + seems to get even better after a day or two.

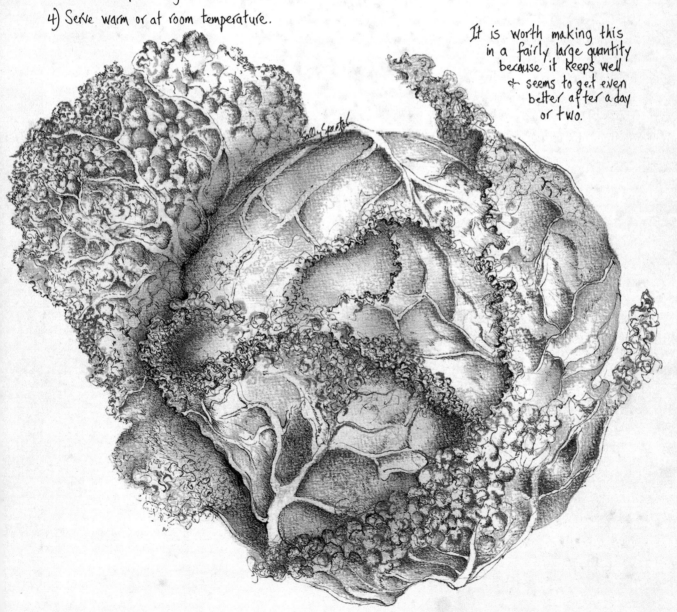

Eggplant MELANZANA melanzana fam. Solanaceae, Solanum melongena

Eggplant is native to western China and northern India: Arabs brought it to Sicily during the Middle Ages and by the 1300's it was being cultivated there and in southern Italy, but the belief that it was poisonous and that eating it caused melancholy and madness hindered its acceptance. Such ideas may explain its name in Italian —MELANZANA probably comes from the Latin MALUM INSANUM, meaning "unhealthy apple." Even when accepted as edible, it was considered difficult to digest and VENTOSO, or windy, that is, gas producing: in Tuscany it is often called PETONCIANO, from the word PETO, meaning fart.

In addition, it was regarded as a "Jewish" food since it was eaten mostly by these people, many Italian Jews having come from the Levant where eggplant is very common; this connection did not help its image although today they are given the credit for introducing it into Venetian cooking, making it another example of this city's ties with the Arab-Byzantine-Greek Eastern Mediterranean world. MELANZANA is still much more present in southern and central than in northern Italy.

Eggplants cultivated in the lagoon are long and narrow or plump and rounded. They are usually purple-black in color but occasionally one sees the smaller violet and white varities; the latter type gave birth to its name in English, from its egg-like shape and color. In Venice, the round variety is grilled or stuffed while the long one is sauteed and used for MELANZANA AL FUNGHETTO, called so because the cooked eggplant resembles certain kinds of cooked mushrooms, or FUNGHI. It is also known as MELANZANA TRIFOLATA: TRIFOLATO refers to any food that is thinly sliced and lightly fried in olive oil, usually with minced garlic and parsley. Much of Venetian cooking is based on using whatever is available to its maximum and very little is thrown away. Thus, there is something almost wanton in the fact that for this recipe, Venetians discard the eggplant's pulp and use only its skin. No doubt in the past it was cooked and eaten separately but today it is usually discarded. The long variety has more skin in proportion to its meat than the round one and is always used when making this dish.

MELANZANE AL FUNGHETTO   SAUTEED EGGPLANT SKINS

~4 SERVINGS~

2 LB. long, thin EGGPLANTS

SALT

OLIVE OIL

2 cloves GARLIC, left whole

2 TB. minced fresh PARSLEY

1) Peel the EGGPLANTS lengthwise, removing long strips of skin with a sharp knife or potato peeler. Cut the strips into thin slices, on the diagonal.

2) Sprinkle the strips with SALT, put them in a colander & put a plate on them. The SALT & weight of the plate help them to release their water content. Leave them this way 30 minutes.

3) In a pan big enough to hold all the SKINS, lightly fry the GARLIC in very little OIL. The GARLIC should color a bit but it must not burn.

4) If the SKINS seem damp, pat them dry before frying them. The smooth skins absorb very little OIL so it should not be necessary to add any to the pan with the GARLIC: too much OIL leaves an unpleasant greasy film on the shiny dark SKINS. Add all the SKINS to the GARLIC & stir well. Cover & cook very gently about 25 minutes. THEY SHOULD NOT BURN. The contents will become very soft & will be significantly reduced in volume.

5) If there is liquid in the pan, continue to cook the SKINS, uncovered, stirring until it evaporates & the mixture becomes "dry". The EGGPLANT SKINS now resemble cooked mushrooms.

6) Sprinkle the SKINS with the PARSLEY. This dish is normally eaten warm or at room temperature.

The tradition of serving this dish as an appetizer with slices of cantalope is said to be a creation of Venetian Jews.

Spices   Spezie

Venetian cooking uses very few spices which often surprises people who closely associate this city with these exotic ingredients and rightly so, for the Republic's great wealth and power were largely due to them. But, they were essentially commodities —imported and exported, bought and sold— more familiar to the traders around the Rialto than to Venetian cooks and housewives and were once far more important for medicine than for gastronomy.

It is believed that spices were an essential part of most ancient societies' sacred rituals and far back in the distant past, Indian and Arab traders began leading caravans of donkeys and camels across India to the Persian Gulf and the Middle East and across the Red Sea to Egypt. These exotic, expensive goods were also used for making such things as cosmetics, love potions, magic elixirs and poisons. The Greek physician, Hippocrates (c. 460-370 B.C.), known as the "father of medicine", wrote of the importance of spices for both medicine and food; the ancient Romans used a great deal of pepper, as well as saffron, ginger, cloves and cardamon and they even

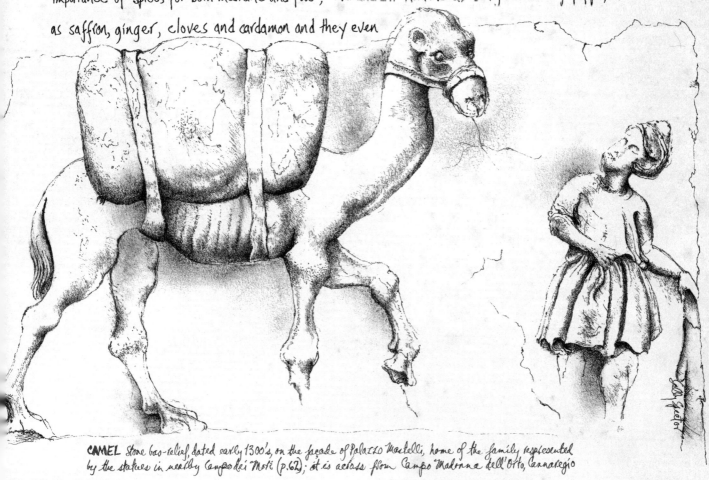

CAMEL stone bas-relief, dated early 1300's, on the façade of Palazzo Mastelli, home of the family represented by the statues in nearby Campo dei Mori (p.62); it is across from Campo Madonna dell'Orto, Cannaregio

scented the stages of their theaters with saffron, cloves and cumin. After that Empire fell in 476, spices seemingly disappeared from Europe, but they did not vanish completely, and Byzantine traders continued to bring Eastern goods to the northern Adriatic, albeit in reduced quantities: for example, a document in the Venetian State Archives cites the donation of a sack of pepper and of incense from a wealthy Venetian to the monastery of Sant'Ilario, located just south of Venice, abandoned in the 1300's when the monks there transfered to San Gregorio, within Venice. This was an exceptional case however, for during the early Middle Ages trade in general was very undeveloped and almost everyone was poor and had difficulty finding enough to eat so there was little demand for such luxuries as spices.

Christian crusaders are thought to have been the first Europeans to "rediscover" a taste for spices when they started going to the Holy Land in the late 11th century for the purpose of waging war against the Moslems in order to take possession of the sacred sites then under their control. Venice created a thriving business out of this religious fervor, thanks to its being the most convenient point for transfering from land to sea transport; in addition to those taking part in the official, organized crusades, for a few hundred years thousands of pilgrims from all over Europe traveled overland as far as Venice and then bought passage on Venetian galleys for the final leg of their journey. Many of these people did not come back, or at least not immediately, and the ships returned filled with tons of precious spices and silks. The Fourth Crusade, in 1204, was particularly significant: Venice persuaded the other participants to detour by way of Constantinople, which they conquered and plundered, opening the way for Venetian ships to sail as far as the Black Sea, where previously only Byzantine, and once in a while Genoese, ships could go. With time, they gained access to other routes and eventually became the middlemen in the exceedingly complex system of the spice trade.

Venetian merchants imported spices in galleys —armed ships, powered by sails and as many as 180 paid oarsmen, not slaves— which were reserved for their most precious cargoes and loaded them on the heavier, less maneuverable, unarmed, round sailing vessels only if they were full or occupied with fighting. Galleys traveled in fleets of as many as ten at a time for mutual protection, using the stars of the night skies to guide them, as had been done since ancient times, until the invention of the magnetic mariner's compass, around 1250. It then became possible to sail during winter months when weather is bad and skies are cloudy, and thus more voyages could be made and more goods transported; in addition, at this time books were compiled listing ports and the distances between them and other landmarks, and scale maps began to be drawn. Venetian traders were present in all of the important commercial centers in Asia and Europe and were recognized as being the most expert in this profession; they reinforced their natural or cultivated talent with language books, at first in manuscript form and then later, printed, which contained words and phrases necessary for bargaining and dealing in, for example, German, Turkish, Greek or Armenian. All of this had an enormous impact on commerce and would eventually also play a role in stimulating the great voyages of exploration and discovery in the late 1400's and in the 1500's, some of which were undertaken for the express purpose of finding new supplies of spices and new trade routes, but in which Venice was no longer a dominant figure.

It is estimated that every year during the 15th century, Venetian galleys brought some 2,500 tons of pepper and ginger, and nearly that much of other spices, from the East, over land and by sea up the Adriatic to the Rialto which was the world's leading spice emporium and probably the best stocked market in general during the Renaissance. Nearly all of the buildings in its vicinity devoted some of the commercial space on their ground floor to dealing in spices or silks which were exported throughout the rest of Europe. Thus, as the great historian of the Mediterranean world, Fernand Braudel (1902-1985) pointed out, considering the changes from one mode of transportation to another, the stops for negotiating passage and paying taxes and duties,

borse per spetie

SPICE BAGS from one of the earliest cookbooks ever published: Opera, by Bartolomeo Scappi (16th cent) first printed in Venice in 1570, by Michiel Tramezino. Scappi, from the Veneto, was the personal chef of Pope Pius the Fifth in Rome. (from the 1570 edition, Correr Library)

sacks of Indian pepper or East Indian cloves had been handled by countless people, and their voyage repeatedly interrupted, before they got to a shop in Germany or England.

This was a highly speculative trade and merchants, agents and anyone else involved in it would go to the Rialto every day for the latest price quotations, a written list of which was distributed daily starting in 1390. Of all the spices, pepper was the most valuable —followed by cinnamon, cloves, ginger, nutmeg and saffron— and grains of it were occasionally used as money, in addition to being the cure-all of early medicine. The State even had its own pepper brokers who used a sort of whisper network for passing information among traders, and eaves-dropping became a valuable skill.

Venice's spice sellers had already formed a corporation by 1258, the SCUOLA DEI SPEZIERI. At first, the differences distinguishing spice sellers, pharmacists and medical doctors were not very precise but in the second half of the 1300's, two separate groups were established: the SPEZIERI DA MEDICINE were pharmacists who prepared and sold syrups, electuaries, balsams and poultices, while the SPEZIERI DA GROSSO sold spices for non-therapeutic use. Both categories were strictly controlled by the State in order to protect the public from fraud, charlatans and harmful or poisonous substances. The spice trade revolutionized the practice of medicine because it multiplied the products available for treating health problems, which previously had been almost completely limited to plants' leaves and roots. Venice's SPEZIERI were famous in all of Italy for their knowledge and skills, much of which were

PERSIAN AMBASSADORS from painting by Gabriele Caliari (1568-1631) "The Doge Marino Grimani Receiving Gifts from the Persian Ambassadors" 1603-5, in the Room of Four Doors in Palazzo Ducale

acquired first hand in the Middle East from accomplished Islamic practitioners.

Spices continued to be used almost exclusively for medicinal purposes in Europe until the end of the Middle Ages when, due mostly to the growth of trade, some people began to get rich: they could buy spices to put in their food and what is sometimes said to be an uncontrollable craving for them was born, especially in the northern countries. This description is somewhat misleading however, because only a tiny minority could actually afford them. Spices became a status symbol, one of the things that distinguished one's social position; poor people used herbs they grew themselves, such as parsley, rosemary and sage, while the rich had pepper, saffron and cloves.

In the 1500's the cuisine of the wealthy was characterized by very strong, pronounced, "spicey" flavors while delicate ones were not appreciated. Various reasons for this have been suggested which none the less leave open the question of whether these preferences were due to necessity or choice: perhaps the pure, natural tastes enjoyed today are a luxury. Since spices were important for medicines they were seen as having healing properties and thus food prepared with them was considered to be particularly fortifying. The ways that food was cooked were well-suited

ROSMARINUM Stecadis facie (ROSEMARY) from De plantis Exoticis Libri Duo by Prospero Alpino (1553-1616) printed posthumously in 1627, in Venice, by Jo. Guerilium

Prospero Alpino was a physician & professor of Pharmacology & Botany at the University of Padua. He believed that travel & research were necessary for doctors so they could learn about the diseases & remedies of countries other than their own. Thus, in 1580, he went to Egypt for 3½ years, with stops in Crete, Corfu & Zante, to study ancient medical treatises, meet doctors & to have direct contact with people of different cultures & of all social classes. He studied the use of herbs & spices in medicine, cultivated exotic plants & for many years was Keeper of the Botanical Garden in Padua, the first of its kind in Europe, founded in 1545. His numerous writings; some of which describe Egyptian medicine & exotic plants, include pieces on how to pronounce sounds in Arabic & transcriptions of that language into Latin. His son carried on his work & edited some of his unpublished books.

to spices: meat and game were usually roasted or stewed, methods that best bring out the flavors of these exotic ingredients. Rich, heavy foods were common and portions tended to be large: spices made them easier to digest. Before the invention of refrigeration in the 19th century, preserving food had always been a problem, resolved to some extent by the processes of drying, salting and smoking, and people often ate things that had "turned" or were spoiled; spices could mask the unpleasant odors of rancid meat, enhance and disguise tastelessness and poor quality, and even help conserve food. Less important, but still worth considering, is the fact that spices broke the monotony imposed by a limited variety of foods and made what there was seem more interesting and delectable. It has also been said that during the Middle Ages, and up to the advent of the so-called Little Ice Age in the late 1400's, Europe's climate may have been warm enough to make spicey food appealing for biochemical and physiological reasons: it encourages perspiration which, as it evaporates, has a pleasing, cooling effect.

All of the above reasons made spices desireable and the fact that they were exotic and precious gave them added allure. Many Venetian traders became very rich from this merchandise but the situation began to change in the 1500's. The discovery, in 1498, of the sea route to India by going around Africa by the Portuguese explorer Vasco da Gama did not immediately affect Venice's hegemony in the spice trade, since Portugal did not succeed in establishing the kind of monopoly that the Republic had created; but, when

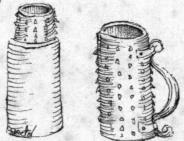

grata noci moschiate

grata zucharo

GRATERS for nutmeg + sugar from Opera ("Work") by Scappi. This cookbook, divided into 6 parts, discusses: the tobats necessary for a cook, how to arrange + use a kitchen, what furniture + utensils it should have, how to recognize good meat + conserve it, etc. There are recipes for fish, vegetables, soups, sweets + the best food for sick people.

Philip II, King of Spain, claimed that country in 1580, he also assumed control of that important commerce which he then lost in the 1600's, when the Dutch and the English attained dominance. Venice gradually lost its possessions in the Eastern Mediterranean and the Venetian traders who had always looked to the East were replaced by new generations who instead, put their energy into undertakings and developments on the mainland, to the West.

In addition to political and economic factors, the use of the spices themselves changed. Medicine was becoming more scientific and with time, chemical remedies were to replace the old ones made from leaves, seeds, bark and sugar. Europeans began drinking coffee, tea and cocoa in the 1600's and these new drinks, whose ingredients, like spices, came from far away places, began to replace them and even became "fashionable." The New World industry of sugar refining made that product cheaper and more easily obtainable: as sweet things became more accessible they came to be preferred to spicey tastes which lost their popularity and importance. The only one of these exotic ingredients that is common in Venetian cooking today is freshly ground pepper, but vestiges of the nearly one hundred SPEZIERI operating here as late as the 1700's are still visible in the form of pharmacies and in place names such as RUGA DEI SPEZIALI and CALLE DEL SPEZIER. The word SPEZIE, like the words spice and species, comes from the Latin word SPECIE, meaning shape, quality, appearance. Thus, these street signs seem to refer not only to the past spice sellers and their shops and merchandise; they also suggest the city itself, the Republic —the SERENISSIMA— whose qualities, appearance and whose very essence were so closely tied to those precious goods.

Sally Spector

SPEZIERE woodcut from Ortus Sanitatis ("Medicinal Garden"), Vol. I, by Irdirio, known as "Tacuinum", printed in Venice in 1511 for Bernardino Benaglia & Giovanni da Cereto. Vol I treats plants, Vol II animals. (from facsimile copy in Marciana Library)

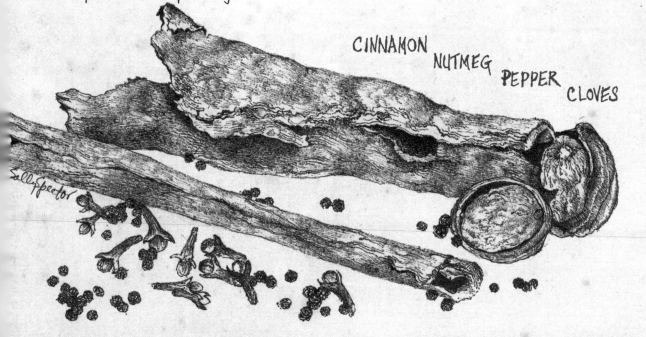

CINNAMON NUTMEG PEPPER CLOVES

Sally Spector

CAMPO SAN STIN & CALLE DEL SPEZIER *The CALLE was named for the spice shop that stood on the corner, on the CAMPO. It later became a pharmacy.*

Sugar & Sweets — Zucchero e Dolci

Of the various flavors that taste buds differentiate, sweetness may be the most pleasurable and probably appeals to people's imagination and fantasy more than others, not only for the sensation it creates on the palate but also because the word itself conveys things fragrant, melodious and delightful. Sweet foods are often associated with festivity, celebration and special occasions; they are not necessary, we do not need them to survive and thus, along with their deliciousness, their attraction no doubt lies in their being part of life's frivolous, ephemeral and indulgent aspects.

Sugar cane is native to India and prior to the 4th century B.C., when people began to make some albeit primitive form of sugar, they merely broke the canes and sucked the pulp out of its stalks like a thick juice. Its Indian origins are seen in the English and Italian words sugar and ZUCCHERO — SUCARO in Venetian— which derive from the Sanskrit SAKHARA, meaning sand or sugar, and it is the source for this word in many other languages as well. (Sanskrit also gave us candy, from KHANDA, a piece of sugar). It is believed that the first Europeans who saw sugar were the troops of Alexander the Great whose trusted Admiral, Nearchus, brought them to the mouths of the Indus River in 324 B.C. Nearchus left a detailed diary and described a 'honey' that grew in reeds without the presence of bees. At that time, honey and fruit provided the rest of the world with sweetness, both figurative and literal: in the Old Testament, the promised land is "flowing with milk and honey" and the ancient Romans made marmelade from apples, pears, figs and honey and made pastries, said to be insipid, from pumpkin. To this day, many Eastern Mediterranean sweets are made with honey, not sugar. Sugar cane was subsequently introduced into Egypt and the Persian Gulf area— Egyptians were the first to purify and refine sugar— and later, Arabs brought it from North Africa into Spain after invading that country in the early 8th century.

Like spices and silk, sugar was to become a very profitable commodity. Venetian merchants began importing it around the year 996 from Syria and Egypt, and it was being grown and refined in North Africa, Spain, Sicily and, in the Eastern Mediterranean, most importantly for Venice, on the island of Cyprus. Venetian traders were extending their activity further and further into this area and beyond, where many Venetians had established residency, and Cyprus' location at the extreme eastern end of the Sea was extremely strategic. A treaty signed with its King in 1306 gave Venice trading rights, lost in 1382 when the Republic's major rival, Genoa, tooked over. But, thanks to sugar and the young Venetian noblewoman, Caterina Cornaro (1451-1510), Venice eventually gained complete control of Cyprus.

The Cornaro family was one of the richest and most important in Venice it produced political and religious leaders as well as successful merchants and its wealth came in great part from the profits their enormous Cyprian sugar plantation rendered. In 1464, the newly crowned but contested King of Cyprus, James II of Lusignano, known as James the Bastard, asked Venice for help in fighting his enemies - Genoa and the Turks, which were also Venice's— and the Cornaro family was able to give him not only a lot of money but also a wife, that is, Caterina, who married him in 1472 after a lengthy engagement period. Bizarre as it may seem, in a subtle act of diplomacy, the Republic officially adopted her and thus, when left a childless widow in 1473, as Queen of Cyprus she was also Venices daughter. Her adoptive parent forced her to abdicate in its favor and Cyprus remained a Venetian possession until 1571 when it was lost to the Turks. Caterina returned to Venice with great pomp and ceremony and was given the town of Asolo, about 80 kms. from Venice, where she lived until the year 1509, often visited by illustrious persons.

VENETIAN MERCHANT IN SYRIA

Woodcut from Habiti antichi et Moderni di tutto il Mondo by Cesare Vecellio (1521-1601). First published in Venice in 1590 by Damian Zenaro, with 420 plates, it is the most famous of over 200 works printed in Europe in the 1500's on clothing. The 2nd edition, printed in Venice in 1598 by Giovanni Bernardo Sessa, contained 500 figures, including subjects from the New World. Vecellio's is the first book with clothes from periods prior to his own (ancient, medieval) & it covers a wider range of countries & society than the others (Europe, Asia, Africa & from rulers to peasants). (From the 1598 edition, Marciana Library)

Control of Cyprus strengthened Venice's political and economic position and although sugar was imported from other places, especially Crete and Egypt, the Cyprian product was considered the best. From the 11th to the 15th century, vast quantities of sacks of crystallized and powdered sugar and cases of sugar loaves were shipped from India and the Middle East, a traffic also stimulated by the Christian crusaders who discovered sugar, or SALE DOLCE, ("sweet salt") in the Holy Land, to the Rialto, which became the world's principal market place for it. At that time, Venetians were not only the most expert of all traders, they were also excellent entrepreneurs and seeing the great profits to be made from sugar, decided to produce it, instead of just buying and selling it. Around 1450, they began importing the raw material and succeeded in perfecting the refining process so as to make a sugar more pure and whiter than ever before. These methods were jealously guarded secrets of the RAFFINATORI, or refiners, who used cloth for filtering, which significantly reduced production time and thus more sugar could be made. As with other things manufactured in Venice, such as glass, candles and soap, whose quality was similarly superior, local artisans had better equipment than their competitors as, for example, the huge copper cauldrons that the highly skilled Venetian metal workers made for boiling sugar.

COMPASS for measuring distances on nautical maps (Correr Museum)

Sally Spector

However much sugar may have been enjoyed for its taste, until the 1600's, when sugar cane began to be cultivated in the New World, its principal use was not culinary, but medicinal. It was used for treating chest ailments and for making syrups – often mixed with almond oil or spices, such as ginger– or sometimes it was put onto hot coals and inhaled; even today, hot, sweet liquids are considered beneficial for coughs and colds and sweet syrups are still used as cough medicine. Sugar was very expensive due to its limited cultivation –it grows only from 37° North to 30° South of the Equator— and its long, complex refining process, and only the wealthy could afford it. Sometimes given in small quantities as a gift, like spices, it was a sign of affluence which even the Venetian Republic exploited to reinforce its image of opulence and power.

The most famous symbolic use of sugar in Venice occurred in 1574 when the State offered a grand banquet in honor of the visit of Henry III (1551-1589), King of Poland, on his way to Paris where he was crowned King of France. Forks, knives, plates, table linens, decorative center-pieces, were all made of sugar and were so realistic that the King, deceived by their likeness, tried to use his sugar napkin which broke in his hands. Such excess was for political, not gastronomic ends and sugar was normally used very sparingly in cooking, such as for the sweet and sour, or AGRO-DOLCE, taste so popular during the Renaissance; sugar was used to season all sorts of food, from fish and meat to soups, and sauces, and was not limited to desserts.

The sugar trade changed dramatically in the 1600's when, after some 2,000 years, the cultivation of sugar moved west, away from the Mediterranean area and into the Atlantic, where not only was the climate perfect for this crop but where there was also plenty of virgin soil, forests to provide fire wood for boiling, and native populations to enslave as cheap labor. Sugar cane started growing on the island of Madeira in the second half of the 1400's and then spread to the Canary Islands; by 1501 it was being harvested on the island of Hispaniola, brought there in 1493 by Christopher Columbus on his second voyage to the New World and it was there, in the West Indies, that it was to have its most profound and tragic effects, both human and environmental. Thousands of people suffered physically and psychologically from the terrible working conditions on the sugar plantations; as this is a one-crop agriculture, more nutritional but less profitable food crops were

ROUND BOTTOMED SHIP from "Pianta Prospettica della Città e delle Lagune" engraved by Bernardo Savioni, printed in Venice by Donato Rasciotti, c.1597. This map of Venice + the lagoons was made to honor the Dogaressa, the wife of the Doge Marino Grimani (1595-1605) from original in Correr Library.

eliminated and massive deforestation irreparably damaged the balance of nature there.

The increased production these new colonies made possible meant that, while great profits were still earned, the price of sugar fell, making it accessible to more people. Demand was increasing: in the mid 1600's coffee and tea were becoming popular and in the 1700's Europeans developed what is described as an insatiable desire, a "madness" for sugar, that led to an ever-growing consumption. Although England and Spain became the dominant sugar producers, Venice's refineries continued to operate until the 1830's. Their importance can be seen in the repeated decrees that the government, always intent on controlling and safeguarding the Republic's most valuable arts and artisans, passed in the 16 and 1700's, prohibiting the RAFFINATORI from leaving Venice to work elsewhere.

Just as the discovery of the New World and the possession of colonies there was to dramatically effect the future of sugar, another event, again completely extraneous to cooking, is usually considered the impetus for significantly changing the sugar industry. The Continental Blockade that the British imposed on Napoleon in the early 1800's cut off France's supply of Caribbean sugar. A substitute was found in the sugar beet, whose sweetening properties had long been recognized; they had been used since antiquity for both medicine and food but how to extract their sugar was not yet understood. Experiments took place in the 16 and 1700's, and in 1801, the first sugar beet factory opened in Silesia. The conflicts between England and France resulted in stimulating interest in this beet, which was bred and perfected, and by 1850, Europe was filling virtually all of its sugar needs with it; although beets are more costly to grow than sugar cane, they tolerate colder climates —Russia is a leading producer— and they have a higher sugar content. In the late 1800's Italy became self-sufficient in terms of sugar production; almost all of its beets grow in the Po Valley area where the flood plain soil is best for this plant. Nearly all of the sugar consumed today comes from beets and it is indistinguishable in taste, sweetness, consistency, appearance and composition from cane sugar.

The origins of many of the typically Venetian sweets made today go back at least 500 years. In 1493, the city's SCALETERI, or pastry cooks, formed an association. The word SCALETTA, or 'little ladder' referred to a thin, wafer-like bread or cracker seasoned with sugar and butter that they made, called that because it resembled the ladder-shaped unleavened bread or PANE AZIMO, AZZIMO in Italian, that Venetian Jews made for the week of Passover, the PASQUA EBRAICA; the word AZZIMO derives from the Greek AZYMOS and the Latin AZYMU which probably come from the Hebrew word MASSAH. The SCALETERI made other simple sweet biscuits and sold them, often in a rather agressive, insistent manner which provoked the government to impose certain restrictions on them: they could not try to lure or tempt customers, they could not cry their wares to attract attention, although this was somewhat permitted at the main markets of Rialto and San Marco, they could not sell inside of churches and they could carry only one basket of sweets around at a time.

Sweets were not, like bread, a necessity and to control excessive consumption of them at festive occasions, which the State called a "PESSIMA ET INHONESTA CONSUETUDINE", or a "very bad and indecent custom", and to limit the drain on flour supplies in the public granaries, the quantity of flour designated for the SCALETERI was restricted. The profession, none the less, was respected and maintained high standards: a minimum of ten years apprenticeship was required, followed by a difficult practical exam, in order to exercise the art of making sweets.

PANE AZIMO This piece of MATZO, made today, is no doubt similar to what gave birth to the term SCALETER, for its resemblance to a SCALA, or ladder. It is made year-round in the GHETO.

Venetian sweets share the same general qualities as the rest of this cuisine: they are simple, uncomplicated, even rustic and may sometimes be overshadowed by the beautiful, more refined DOLCI from other places in Italy that are now available here.

Ironically, what may be the most famous dessert associated with Venice today

TIRA MI SU, is not "Venetian" and is a quite recent creation. Many of Venice's typical sweets are cookies and often contain ingredients that reflect the two aspects that most characterize this city's past — the sea and the land, raisins and pine nuts and spices from the East, and corn-meal from the mainland to the West. Certain sweets are made only for specific holidays, such as Carnival, the feast day of St. Martin and Christmas, and are sometimes similar to those elsewhere in Italy. While today Venetians are probably more "national" in their dessert choices than in the rest of the meal, usually preferring rice and fish instead of pasta and meat, they still often finish with their traditional BISCOTTI, dipped in sweet wine.

I remember my original surprise when, at the end of a scrumptious dinner, prepared from scratch by the hostess, she served a store-bought dessert and it was clear that this in no way detracted from her skills or the success of her cooking. Dinner parties here, whether spectacular and elaborate or simple and modest, rarely finish with homemade sweets. Some-times, guests bring a dessert instead of the usual bottle of wine which means that, if it is a surprise and a sweet was already planned, both of them are served.

The following pages are devoted to some of Venice's most traditional sweets.

BAICOLO

This thin, dry cookie was created in Venice in the 1700's by a certain Colussi and named BAICOLO because its oval form is like that of the lagoon's bass and grey mullet fish when they are very young, and called BAICOLI. The word probably derives from BAIOCCOLO, which was a small Roman coin of little value and was used to describe young things that have less value than the adult. The simplicity of its appearance and ingredients — flour, yeast, sugar, butter and water are rather deceiving since, while it is not technically difficult to make them, it requires three days and a lot of kneading: prepared in stages, the dough is left to rise twice ; once baked, it is left to sit for two days, then thinly sliced and the slices are all laid flat on cookie sheets and rebaked. There are no variations in the BAICOLO — it is unique. It is industrially produced by one company, called Colussi, and sold in small boxes and larger tins, in which they can be kept for several months, and even expert cooks agree that there is no reason to make them since the commercial product is so good. Some bakers in Venice sell FONDI DI BAICOLI by weight: they are the slightly rounded ends of the long rolls which are not included with the packaged, uniformly thin slices. BAICOLI are often dipped in hot chocolate, tea, sweet wine or ZABAIONE, a custom that was very popular in the 18th century and still present today in spite of the great variety of other sweets that have become available in the past 30 years here.

BAICOLI are sometimes described as being the famous PAN BISCOTI, the special biscuits that the Republic made for its navy, but it is more likely that the BAICOLO was merely inspired by them. PAN BISCOTI were a sort of cracker with the amazing quality of being completely immune to worms and insect larvae and, in addition, were extremely nutricious and tasty. Even the FRISOPI — the crumbs and any residue left over from making this precious food — were gathered and used to make soup on board ship for the sailors. The government starting making them in 1335; State authority was required for making them and they could be made only in the ovens of the Arsenale, the State's shipyard. They were so remarkable that foreign countries bought them from the Republic for their armies. Their recipe has never been found nor has the secret of their preservation been discovered, but, in addition to being baked twice, as the very word 'biscuit' indicates, in order to reduce their moisture, they probably contained potato and corn starch as well as the best quality wheat flour available. Proof of their extraordinary resistence was established in 1821, although already well-known, when some PAN BISCOTI were found, in perfect condition, on Crete, called Candia by the Venetians. The Republic had ceded this island to the Turks in 1669 so it is presumed that the BISCOTI had been there for at least 152 years.

~10-12 SERVINGS~   7 EGGS   13 TB. SUGAR

13 oz. MASCARPONE, a rich, soft sweet-cream cheese

1½ cups strong black COFFEE

2/3 cup MARSALA

about 60 LADY FINGER or SAVOY COOKIES

2 TB. powdered bitter CHOCOLATE

1) Separate the EGG
   WHITES + YOLKS into two
   bowls. Add the SUGAR to the
   YOLKS & whip 'til foamy. With a
   wooden spoon, stir in the MASCARPONE.

2) Beat the EGG WHITES 'til they form
   peaks & add them to the MASCARPONE, stirring
   'til it has a uniform, fluffy consistency.

3) Combine the COFFEE & MARSALA in a bowl.
   Quickly dip the COOKIES in the liquid – they
   should not get soggy or fall apart. Cover the
   bottom of a shallow rectangular pan with a
   layer of moistened COOKIES & spread a layer of
   the EGG mixture over them, then another layer
   of COOKIES, alternating 'til there is nothing left.
   Finish with a layer of the EGG mixture. Cover
   with plastic & put in the refrigerator at least two
   hours; it can be eaten immediately, but most people
   serve it chilled.

4) Before eating, sprinkle the TIRAMISÙ with
   powdered bitter CHOCOLATE.

Sally Spector

TIRAMISÙ

This dessert, born in the Veneto after World War II, includes coffee & cacao, two "exotic" ingredients which Venice was in part responsible for introducing to Europeans.

There are many variations of it: this recipe is for the original, authentic "PICK-ME-UP", or TIRA-MI-SÙ cake.

CALIE DEL SCALETER

RIO DE SAN TROVASO, DORSODURO

PINZA   NICOLOTTA

PINZA in Italian means pliers, tongs, pinchers and forceps. In Venice, PINZA is also a sweet: heavy, nourishing and filling, it is more a snack than a dessert. There are numerous variations of it but the theme common to all is the use of white and yellow —wheat and corn— flour. Virtually all recipes also call for raisins and eggs, while their differences lie in the amounts and proportions of these ingredients and in the choice of the optional ones, which include : pine nuts, candied fruit, chopped dried figs, almonds, fennel seeds, grated lemon or orange peel, powdered cinnamon and powdered cloves. Baked in a rectangular or square pan, it is about one inch high and sold in pieces or slices by weight; it may, but need not, be eaten with a fork and is normally consumed at room temperature, not hot. The top is caramel-colored, its interior is yellow and speckled with raisins, etc. It was once traditional to eat PINZA on the 6th of January for the FESTA DELLA BEFANA, or EPIFANIA, when Italian children received gifts as are given in other countries, and now Italy, for Christmas.

As simple and rustic as PIN-ZA may seem today, and it is considered a "poor" sweet, one of its important ingredients -raisins- was once precious and exotic. They came from Venice's possessions in the Ionian Sea, especially from the island of Zante, or Zakinthos, under Venetian domain from 1489-1797, where grapes were grown expressly for being dried into

raisins, or UVETTA, UETA in Venetian —"little grapes"— also called UVA PASSA and UVA SECCA. A very profitable commodity, they were shipped in great quantity from there to Venice and on to England in the 1500's, used to make plum pudding: in 1566, a ship's entire cargo consisted of just raisins from Zante -1,000 barrels of them- which its Venetian owners

Unidentified stone bas-relief of a ship & its cargo of barrels. The two 'Evil Eyes' on its prow, once a common feature of ships were to protect its crew from danger. At: SOTOPORTEGO of Calle de le Acque, near Church of San Salvador, S. Marco.

exported to northern Europe.

Related to PINZA is something called NICOLOTTA, named after one of Venice's oldest and most famous working class neighborhoods, San Nicolò dei Mendigoli, or MENDICANTI, meaning beggars. This area, populated mostly by fishermen and humble craftsmen, had an even stronger identity than in other parts of Venice as well as their own particular traditions. Residents would elect one of the best fishermen to be their official representative, the DOGE DEI NICOLOTTI, who was received by the real Doge in Palazzo Ducale and who was an important figure in the life of this community. Thus, it is not surprising that a Venetian food, now eaten by everyone here, has this name. It differs from PINZA in that it is made with stale bread instead of cornmeal.

PINZA
preheat oven to 350°

{
16 OZ. WHITE FLOUR
8 OZ. yellow CORN FLOUR } proportions may vary)

7 OZ. SUGAR   2 OZ. BUTTER   A }

4 OZ. RAISINS *   pinch of SALT
}

{
2 beaten EGGS   ½ cup MILK   B }

small glass of GRAPPA or SWEET WINE
}

Combine the dry ingredients. (A) + add (B). Mix well 'til the dough has a uniform consistency. CORN FLOUR absorbs a lot of moisture; if necessary, add more MILK. Put in a greased baking tin & bake about 40 minutes: when a toothpick stuck into it comes out clean, it is done.

✳ Choose one or more of the optional ingredients on the preceding page; use amounts equal to or less than the quantity of RAISINS. If FIGS are added, less sugar may be used.

PINZA may be made in a variety of forms as seen here.

NICOLOTTA
preheat oven to 375°

16 oz. stale BREAD - broken into pieces

1 QT MILK   4 OZ. WHITE FLOUR

2 OZ. BUTTER   4 OZ. SUGAR

1-4 beaten EGGS   small glass WHITE WINE

3 OZ. RAISINS *   1-2 TB. FENNEL SEEDS

pinch of SALT   1-2 TB. BREAD CRUMBS

Soak the BREAD in the MILK until soft. Stir in the FLOUR. Add the other ingredients, mixing well to make a firm, uniform dough. Grease a baking tin, sprinkle it with BREAD CRUMBS & spread the dough over them. Bake about 1 hour.

Sally Spector

BUSSOLÀ

I consider this one of the world's best cookies though its name and appearance give little hint of its extraordinary taste and texture. Its name derives from the Venetian word BUSA — BUCA in Italian, meaning hole or opening; it is also called BURANELLO, like the natives of the island of Burano where it was born. A few decades ago, the owner of a famous restaurant there asked a local baker to make a BUSSOLÀ that he could offer his clients to eat with, and dip into, sweet wine for dessert. Thus, the ESSE was created, named for its "S" shape. Today, both these cookies come in a variety of shapes, sizes and thicknesses and are made in Venice as well as being industrially produced on the terra firma. None, however, are as good   as the ones baked out in the lagoon.

The BUSSOLÀ is perfect for dunking in hot tea or sweet wine which it absorbs without disintegrating, but it is also wonderful to munch on all by itself; as seen by its ingredients, it is extremely nourishing and filling. If kept in an airtight container, this cookie stays good for a few months though it may get a bit hard.

already mixed at home, or all the raw ingredients, to the island's bakers who prepare the BUSSOLÀ and bake them in their bread ovens, to be picked up a few hours later. Household ovens cannot produce an authentic BUSSOLÀ.

The BUSSOLÀ is not made at home, or at least not completely. Today, as in the past, BURANELLI who do not want to buy them, bring the dough,

Bussolai are available all year long nowadays but they were traditionally made only for Easter, when people would wait in line for their turn at the bakers'. For this holiday they contain more egg yolks than during other months, for spiritual rather than gastronomic reasons, since the egg is a symbol of resurrection, and these cookies are even softer and tastier than usual. It is easy to sympathize with the nuns in the convent of San Maffio (Matthew, or Matteo in Italian) on Mazzorbo, the island that today is joined to Burano by a bridge: a document in the Venetian State Archives from the 1500's records that they were ordered to reduce the amount they spent for BUSSOLAI as it was thought they were overindulging in them. The convent of San Maffio was founded in 1298, suppressed by Napoleon in 1806 and destroyed soon thereafter.

2 LB. 3 OZ. WHITE FLOUR

1 LB. 5 OZ. SUGAR

12 EGG YOLKS

11 OZ. BUTTER

1/2 tsp. VANILLA EXTRACT

grated peel of 1 LEMON

Preheat oven to 400°. If possible, bake in a brick bread oven.

Mix the FLOUR + SUGAR together + make a "well" in the center. Pour in the EGG YOLKS + mix well. Add the BUTTER + the VANILLA + continue to work the dough 'til it takes on a uniform consistency + is quite soft + malleable. Make circles or "S" forms or what-

ever shape is preferred. The BUSOLA may be from 2 to 8 inches in diameter, made from a strip of dough whose ends are joined to make a circle. The ESSE is usually about 4 inches long, to be dunked in something. Bake on greased cookie sheets for about 15 minutes.

ZALETO

The ZALETO is named for its yellow color —ZALO in Venetian, GIALLO in Italian— which comes from the corn flour in it. It probably originated around Belluno, some 100 kms. north of Venice, and in the Friuli region to the east, both once extremely poor areas where the introduction of corn in the 1600's greatly improved the local diet. It is said that a water mill grinds corn to a finer consistency than other types of mills and water is what turned the mills in these two places. The high quality corn flour thus produced was used to make these cookies, which were sold in Venice by street vendors who also peddled them from door to door. Today ZALETI are available in pastry and bread shops, easily recognized by their distinctive shape —an elongated oval tapered at its ends— and color. ZALETI are made in many parts of the Veneto and similar cookies can also be found in Central Italy; as the ZALETO moves south its ingredients are enriched to include pine nuts, almonds and chopped dried figs.

Preheat oven to 350°

9 OZ. BUTTER   9 OZ. SUGAR

pinch of SALT   5 EGGS

12 OZ. WHITE FLOUR
12 OZ. YELLOW CORN FLOUR

9 OZ. RAISINS - soaked in tepid water a few minutes to soften

Cream together the BUTTER, SUGAR & SALT. Beat in the EGGS, one at a time, & then stir in the FLOUR & the RAISINS. The dough should have a solid, uniform consistency. Form the ZALETI by hand: the traditional cookie is about 3 inches long & tapered at both ends but it can be made larger or smaller, according to personal preference. Bake on greased cookie sheets for about 15 minutes.

ZALETI are sometimes lightly sprinkled with powdered sugar after baking, while still warm.

FUGASSA

The Venetian word FUGASSA —FOCACCIA in Italian— comes from FOCOLARE, meaning hearth or fireplace. The FUGASSA is a sweet yeast bread, circular in shape, about three inches high with a puffy rounded top which is sometimes dotted with sugar. It belongs to a large family of food born in the remote past; derived from ordinary, everyday, life-sustaining bread, the FOCACCIA was created to celebrate a special occasion and thus a sense of ritual and symbolism is associated with it. Every part of Italy has a characteristic sweet bread made to commemorate events such as lings, baptisms, Christmas and Easter; in a few places the FOCACCIA is not a sweet bread but rather, a salty flat one made with olive oil — it is also called SCHIACCIATA, meaning squeezed or squashed. The Venetian FUGASSA is lighter and has a more delicate flavor than that in other areas: it contains flour, yeast, sugar, butter, milk, eggs and a bit of grated lemon rind. Once this was traditional for Easter but is now eaten all year round. Rarely made at home, Venetians take advantage of the numerous SCALETERI here renowned for their excellent FUGASSE.

CROCCANTE

CROCCANTE is a toasted almond version of peanut brittle. It is often served, like the ESSE cookie, at the end of a meal, with sweet wine. Some bars keep them in a glass jar on the counter, to be sold by the piece, and they are usually available at stands that offer the numerous types of hard and soft nougats, toffees and carmelized sweets made in most regions of Italy.

BISCOTTO DI SAN MARTINO

A gaily decorated cookie in the form of a horse and rider fills Venetian pastry and bread shop windows every year for the 11th of November, the feast day of the 4th century soldier saint, Martin of Tours, famous for having given half of his cloak to a naked beggar. But there is also a pagan aspect to this holiday: it celebrates the end of the farming season when the fall harvest is finished and most agricultural activity rests until the following spring. L'ESTATE DI SAN MARTINO — St. Martin's summer— is Indian Summer, a short period of exceptionally mild weather that often occurs in mid-November.

Index

English words: black ink, lower case letters
Italian words: black ink, capital letters

Venetian words: gray ink, lower case letters
Recipes: gray ink, capital letters with asterisk ✳

Selected Bibliography

AA. VV., _Storia della cultura veneta_, Vicenza 1976-1986

AA. VV., _Storia di Venezia_, Istituto della Enciclopedia Italiana con la collaborazione scientifica della Fondazione Giorgio Cini, Roma 1991-1996

AGOSTINI, Pino - ZORZI, Alvise, _A tavola con i Dogi. Storia e ricette della grande cucina veneziana_, Venezia 1991

ASPIV, _L'acquedotto di Venezia_, Venezia 1984

BALLARINI, Giovanni, _Il latte e la vita_, Milano 1994

BELTRAMI, Daniele, _Saggio di storia dell'agricoltura nella repubblica di Venezia durante l'età moderna_, Vicenza 1955

BORGNINO, G. Camillo, _Cenni storico-critici sulle origini dell'industria dello zucchero in Italia_, Bologna 1910

BRAUDEL, Fernand, _The Mediterranean and the Mediterranean World in the Age of Phillip II_, London-New York 1972

BRIANTA, Donata, "Il riso tra stato e mercato" in _Storia dell'agricoltura italiana in età contemporanea_, vol. III, pp. 123-188, Venezia 1991

BUONASSISI, Vincenzo, _Il nuovo codice della pasta_, Milano 1985

CAMPORESI, Piero, Introduzione e note (a cura di) in Pellegrino Artusi, _La scienza in cucina e l'arte di mangiar bene_, Torino 1970

Id., _Alimentazione, Folclore, Società_, Parma 1980

COLTRO, Dino, _Mondo contadino: società, lavoro, feste e riti agrari del lunario veneto_, Venezia 1982

DIANA, Aldo, _Il rifornimento idrico di Venezia insulare_, Venezia 1959

DOSI, A. - SCHNELL, F., _I romani in cucina_, Roma 1986

FALASSI, Alessandra, "Il percorso del risotto" in _Cucina cultura società_, pp. 119-122, atti del Convegno Scientifico Internazionale (Passariano), Bologna 1982

LANE, Frederic C., _The Collected Papers of Frederic C. Lane_, Baltimore 1966

Id., _Venice, A Maritime Republic_, Baltimore 1973

LISINI, Alessandro, _La forchetta da tavola_, Siena 1911

LUZZATTO, Gino, _Storia economica dell'età moderna e contemporanea_, Padova 1934

Id., _Storia economica di Venezia dall' XI al XVI secolo_, Venezia 1961

MARANGONI, Giovanni, _Le associazioni di mestiere nella repubblica veneta (vittuaria - farmacia - medicina)_, Venezia 1974

MESSEDAGLIA, Luigi, _Notizie storiche sul mais, una gloria veneta_, Venezia 1924

Id., _Il mais e la vita rurale italiana_, Piacenza 1927

MILANI VIANELLO, Daniela, _Gli scaletteri_, Venezia 1991

MINTZ, Sidney, _Sweetness and Power: The Place of Sugar in Modern History_, New York 1985

MONTANARI, Massimo L'alimentazione contadina nell'alto Medioevo, Napoli 1979

MORGANTI, Paolo, Il radicchio rosso di Treviso, Treviso 1995

NICCOLI, Vittorio, Saggio storico e bibliografico dell'agricoltura italiana dalle origini al 1900, Torino 1902

ROSA SALVA, Paolo, Laguna e pesca, Venezia 1975

SALAMAN, Redcliffe Nathan, The History and Social Influence of the Potato, Cambridge 1949

SALTINI, Antonio, Storia delle scienze agrarie, Bologna 1984-1987

SALVATORI de ZULIANI, Mariù, A tola co i nostri veci, la cucina veneziana, Milano 1987

Scopritori e Viaggiatori del Cinquecento e del Seicento, vol. I: Il Cinquecento, a cura di
     Ilaria Luzzana Caraci, Milano-Napoli 1991 (la letteratura italiana - storia e testi)

SENTIERI, Maurizio - ZAZZU, Guido, I semi dell'Eldorado. L'alimentazione in Europa dopo la
     scoperta dell' America, Bari 1992

SOMOGYI, Stefano, "L'alimentazione nell' Italia unita" in Storia d' Italia, vol. V, pp. 841-887
     Torino 1973

TANNAHILL, Reay, Food in History, New York 1988

TASSINI, Giuseppe, Curiosità veneziane ovvero: origini delle denominazioni stradali, Venezia 1979

TUCCI, Ugo "L'alimentazione a bordo delle navi veneziane" in Studi veneziani, N.S. XIII, Venezia 1987

VIANELLO, Gianfranco, Racconti di un pescatore: la laguna di Venezia prima dell' inquinamento,
     Venezia 1993

WEATHERWAX, Paul, The Story of the Mais Plant, Chicago 1923

ZORZI, Elio, Osterie veneziane, Venezia 1967

Enciclopedia Agraria Italiana, Roma 1952

All of the drawings were done expressly for this book and were executed in pen and ink
and/or pencil; the color was added with pastel, colored pencil and water color. Scenes of
Venice and drawings after Venetian monuments and sculpture were done from life (except pages
117 and 131), as were the drawings of food, while those after paintings were done from
photographs. Illustrations copied from old woodcuts and engravings were done in the
Marciana Library, the Correr Library and the Querini-Stampalia Library, in Venice, using books
—mostly original editions— in their collections. Other subjects, such as agricultural
equipment, scale models, etc., were drawn from examples found in various places in the
Veneto; their location is indicated in the descriptions accompanying the drawings.